SH*T THEY DIDN'T TELL YOU

HOW TO SUCCEED IN THE CREATIVE INDUSTRIES

by PAUL WOODS

LAURENCE KING PUBLISHING

First published in Great Britain in 2021 by
Laurence King Student & Professional
An imprint of Quercus Editions Ltd
Carmelite House
50 Victoria Embankment
London EC4Y 0DZ

An Hachette UK company

Text and illustrations © Paul Woods 2021

A CIP catalogue record for this book is available
from the British Library

ISBN 978 1 78627 953 8

10 9 8 7 6 5 4 3 2 1

Commissioning editor: Liz Faber
Senior editor: Gaynor Sermon
Design: TurnbullGrey

Printed and bound in China

Laurence King Publishing is committed to ethical
and sustainable production. We are proud participants
in The Book Chain Project ®
bookchainproject.com

CONTENTS

FOREWORD

Loving something, even being good at it, doesn't ensure success. This is a lesson many designers, including myself, had to learn the hard way. I didn't know it at the time, but when I graduated from ArtCenter College of Design with a BFA in graphic design, I thought I was well prepared. In fact, I remember not paying attention during my marketing/sales class. I had this belief that marketing and self promotion were a way to compensate for a weak portfolio. I know how foolish and arrogant that sounds, yet that's what I thought at the time.

My portfolio, by my estimation, was good enough to get me work, or so I thought. So I skipped portfolio preparation class and didn't sign up for a single on-campus interview.

Just a few months after graduation, I had the opportunity to start my own company, so I did. I registered a company name, opened a checking account, got a business license, paid my fees and was off to the races. Except... nothing happened. Crickets. No one called. No one cared. I quickly learned that I was a tiny, insignificant fish, lost in a giant ocean. It was a humbling experience.

I later realized that it took a lot more than a portfolio to be successful. You need the right mix of focus, exposure, guidance, relationships, business acumen, resources and a little bit of luck to run a design business.

"If you fail to plan, you are planning to fail."—Benjamin Franklin

Sadly, I didn't even know where to start. Who do I call? What do I ask? Where do I go? I did the best I could, and made up the rest as I went along. It was like trying to solve a Rubik's cube in the dark, with one hand. Unsurprisingly, the first two years in business were the hardest of my life—filled with lost pitches, long hours of work and little financial reward. It felt like every decision I made led me down an inevitable path of failure, embarrassment and lost opportunity.

It was like trying to solve a Rubik's cube in the dark, with one hand.

It sounds painful. I know. That's because it was. For those who are reading this, you'll come to quickly realize that Paul has written something quite special—a business/marketing guide for creatives.

Business books are dry and dense, and tend to over-explain concepts with theories that are not applicable for most creatives. Design books, though rich with inspiration, are usually light on practical advice. Seeing what others do rarely leads to *doing* what they do.

Sh*t They Didn't Tell You is a seriously fun, straight-talking, highly potent book of ideas, written from the vantage point of someone who has been in the trenches and lived to tell about it.

Paul has managed to write an honest, sincere, and easy-to-digest book about the business of design. It's full of super-smart advice, whimsical illustrations, useful diagrams, and flow charts to help you make the best decisions in alignment with who you are, and covers a range of topics, like how to: create a portfolio that doesn't suck, present your work, deal with clients, and find a job you love (to name a few).

> Wouldn't it be great to do work that you love, for people you care about, and companies you believe in?

Wouldn't it be great to do work that you love, for people you care about, and companies you believe in? Isn't that the whole reason why you got into design in the first place? Yeah. Me too!

This book is the book I wish I'd had (and read) when I was embarking on my career. Sit back, dig in, and apply what you learn. You'll save yourself from committing the same silly and totally unnecessary mistakes I made.

Chris Do
Entrepreneur, designer, teacher, and speaker
The Futur

PREFACE

When I left design school in 2010, I was more than a little lost. In the months immediately after my graduate show, I fell into a deep funk, unsure of myself, the type of work I should be doing, and the prospective career path in front of me. I flunked several job interviews, gained about 30 pounds, and spent the bulk of six months in a state of existential uncertainty that would make even Kanye West proud. In short, I had no idea where to start.

There is a general unawareness of the breadth of perks that a creative career can really offer you.

This feeling of uncertainty is common for those starting out in the creative industries, and no wonder. Even with the rise of online learning and the democratized sharing of knowledge, the gap between creative education and the "real world" is substantial. Young creatives starting out are largely unprepared for what to expect and the skills they actually need. Perhaps more importantly, there is a general unawareness of the breadth of perks that a creative career can really offer you.

When I started out, I had no idea about—well, anything, really. I didn't know how much I should charge for my work. I didn't know I needed a good accountant, or a lawyer, for that matter. I didn't know that it was possible to get paid to travel and live around the world (in my case, London, Berlin, New York, and Los Angeles). I certainly didn't know that it was possible to get rich being a designer. And I didn't know that sometimes, just sometimes, creative work can change the world. This, dear reader, is the shit they—your peers, your professors, your co-workers, and even your mom—didn't tell you.

Think of this book as a pocket guide to help you plan your stops along the way.

Looking back, what I really needed was a guide to help me find my way in the industry. Not just another "business-for-creatives" book, but something more akin to a travel guide that laid out the options in front of me and helped me make the right decisions. Something that was simple, visual, and perhaps even fun. A guide that made planning those tricky first steps of one's career more like planning a travel adventure.

After searching high and low, I realized that no such book existed. It is for that reason that you, dear reader, are reading these words today. Think of this book as a pocket guide to help you plan your stops along the way. Perhaps you want to work at an agency in a big city on the other side of the world? Maybe you want to get paid to travel the world as a freelancer? Your passion might lie in a more noble pursuit, such as using your talents to change the world through a social cause. Or perhaps—and most likely—you don't really know yet, and just need a map to help you navigate your course. You've come to the right place. Over these 144 pages, I hope things will become a little clearer.

Enough blabbering from me. Let's get started.

Paul Woods

After searching high and low, I realized that no such book existed. It is for that reason that you, dear reader, are reading these words today.

TAKE A MOMENT, MAKE A PLAN

It's the morning after your graduate show. Lying among a sea of bottles from the night before with an unrelenting hammer inside your brain that refuses to stop thumping, you attempt to pull yourself together. A wave of anxiety threatens to swallow you up as the greatest existential question of all raises its head: Where do I start? And with that, you realize that the party is over, and the real world beckons. Shit.

THE POST-GRADUATION PANIC

Uncertainty. Anxiety. Existential doubt. No, I'm not talking about the latest episode of *Keeping Up with the Kardashians*. I am, of course, referring to the post-graduation crisis, a rather nasty condition that almost everyone experiences at the start of their career.

Without question, the months following graduation are among the most difficult times of your professional career. You've gone from the warm and safe confines of university—a cozy place where you constantly had the ear and interest of your professors and peers—to the cold reality of a world that gives zero fucks about you. Your professors have moved onto the next fresh batch of final-year students and you are older news than a slice of pie that's been sitting out in the sun for too long. You are on your own. It is like being slapped with a cold, wet fish.

The months following graduation are among the most difficult times of your professional career.

As a means of reassurance, I will tell you this: The postgraduate panic affects everyone, regardless of talent, networking ability, or grades. In 2010, I graduated near the top of my class, won a rather handsome collection of student awards, and was the apple of my professors' collective eyes. The day after our graduate show, I was just as much on my own as every other graduate scrambling for a first-round interview for an internship, let alone a full-time job. I was entirely unprepared for the real world, and I fell into a severe funk for about six months until I moved to London. In fact, it took me a couple of years to regain the confidence from my university days. Don't fret, dear reader. This is part of everyone's career, and those of us with a creative disposition are even more prone to it.

So, what can you do about the post-graduation panic? The answer is: quite a lot, actually. Now is the time to get organized and make a plan to conquer the world. Or, at the very least, make a plan to get out of your hungover state.

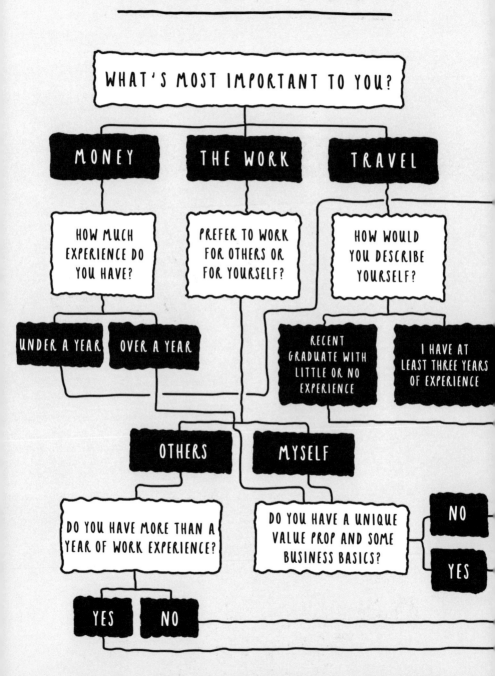

LOOK FOR A JOB

The "classic" route: Finding a job you love at an agency or studio. A great way to start your career.

DO AN INTERNSHIP

For those lacking in experience or network, an internship is a great way to get your foot in the door.

FURTHER STUDY

A good route to build your network or if you need to find your creative voice or grow your business skills.

REMOTE FREELANCE

If you have no job offers, but still want to get paid to travel, consider freelancing remotely for home clients.

START YOUR OWN BUSINESS

If you're after money, starting your own business has the highest return (and risk) on investment.

HAVE YOU ALREADY TRIED LOOKING FOR A JOB ABROAD WITH NO SUCCESS?

YES   NO

THE IMPORTANCE OF A PLAN

Every great creative career starts with two clear steps: Create a long-term goal and put in place the tasks you need to make it happen. It's not rocket science. Think of planning your career as like planning a trip abroad. You wouldn't start without doing at least a little research, picking a destination, and buying your plane tickets. Sure, the details of each place you may stop at along the way will change—after all, the best experiences are usually the most unexpected ones—but you need to start somewhere.

> Every great creative career starts with two clear steps: Create a long-term goal and put in place the tasks you need to make it happen.

Now, before you enter a second wave of panic of "But Paul, I have absolutely no idea what I want to do...," realize that everyone—and I do mean everyone—feels like this. Even your smart-ass classmate who just snagged an internship with the fancy creative shop down the street. They don't have a clue either. If it seems as if they do, they're just pretending.

No matter what is presented to you after you graduate, you must accept the importance of a plan. Without a plan, your work, your career, and your life will end up where others want it to go, rather than where you want it to go. Keep in mind that you don't have to stick to a plan forever, but when you're starting out, having an end point to work toward will help to direct your focus until you find your feet.

MAKING YOUR PLAN

OK, ready to shrug off the grad-show hangover and make your plan? Great. Let's start with these steps:

STEP ONE: THINK BIG. NOW THINK BIGGER
All too often, creatives in the early years of their careers play it safe: They think small. Time and time again, I have seen the most talented young creatives undersell themselves out of lack of confidence, and then settle for an unpaid corporate internship in their hometown of Shitsville. Remember, if you start your career in Shitsville, it doesn't get any easier to leave Shitsville when you get older.

Remember this: At the start of your career you have nothing to lose. Never again in your entire career will you be in such a luxurious position. You do not have a reputation to ruin, a job to be fired from, or any expectations of you of any kind. Enjoy this anonymity, the fact that this is the moment when you are expected to fail again, again, and again, at least a dozen more times for good measure.

Now, open your mind and think bigger. Instead of thinking about where you can scrape a first internship, consider the big picture: Get paid to travel the world. Snag a mentorship with one of your heroes. Work at the biggest film studio in Los Angeles. Travel to New York and become a fashion photographer. Be bold. Be courageous. Now is the time and life is short.

Repeat: You. Have. Nothing. To. Lose.

STEP TWO: CREATE YOUR STATEMENT OF INTENT
Now it's time to get specific and create your long-term goal. In order to help you transform a vague idea into an actionable goal, you will now create your "statement of intent". This is a clear expression of your goal in one single sentence. Be as specific as possible with your statement, and add a timeframe.

For example:
- "Within three years, I will be working at a major design agency in Europe."
- "By the end of this year, I will be working as a freelance designer in Amsterdam."
- "I will be a design lead at a Silicon Valley tech company in five years."

GOOD PLANNING

Has a clear
career goal
written down

Has a growing and
well-maintained
spreadsheet of
contacts

Only reaches
out to places she
actually wants
to work for

Understands
the importance
of business
basics

Does not reek of
desperation, or gin

As cool as a
fucking cucumber

NO PLANNING

THINK BIGGER!

YOU HAVE NOTHING TO LOSE

When you have this statement, take a large sheet of paper, write it down, and hang it prominently on a wall in your home. This is your goal, and your constant reminder to keep you on track. Planning your career for the first time is a major endeavor that will consume your life for months. Believe me, when you are knee-deep in job applications or travel plans, or frustrated by the 700th form you need to complete for a work visa, you will need a reminder of why you're doing it.

Planning your career for the first time is a major endeavor that will consume your life for months.

When I made the decision to move to New York, I had had the words "By the end of this year I will move to New York to work in an ad agency" hanging in my living room for months. It sounds silly, but it worked. Within four months of penning the statement of intent, all my belongings were packed into a freight container on their way to the Big Apple.

STEP THREE: PRIORITIZE THE FIRST FIVE STEPS TO REACH THAT GOAL

Your statement of intent is your high-level goal, but without spelling out actionable steps to get there, it's as much a pipedream as me delivering the manuscript for this book to my publisher on time.

In this exercise, you will detail the necessary steps to achieve your goal. However, as you are probably aware, humans do not possess the ability to predict the future. Don't waste time mapping out the 427 steps you will complete over the next eleven years. Map out as many as you can, then prioritize the list. Now focus on the top five only. Once you've finished them, reassess your list and tackle the next five.

A helpful tool to create and manage this list is a "Kanban" board, which is an agile project-management tool that allows you to look at work in progress and maximize efficiency within your team. There are four very simple columns:

- Backlog: A prioritized list of all items in your list
- To do: The top five things you will focus on immediately
- Doing: Tasks in progress
- Done: Completed tasks

This list can be made of Post-its on your wall, or you can use a digital tool such as Trello if you're feeling fancy. Make a fixed timeslot once a week when you go through the ritual of reviewing and reprioritizing your list.

STEP FOUR: COMMUNICATE YOUR PLAN

The trick to getting shit done is holding yourself accountable to someone other than yourself. Announce your plan to your family and friends, and even to the trolls on social media. Ensure that if you do procrastinate in waddlesome sloth for six months, you are at least accountable to somebody—or they'll poke fun at you.

STEP FIVE: BE READY TO FOLLOW THE OPPORTUNITIES

Rejoice! You now have a plan. But before you depart to the land of slumber to fend off your grad-show hangover, one more thing. No matter how meticulous your plan, you must be ready to abandon it when the right opportunity presents itself. The very best opportunities have a habit of presenting themselves at the most inconvenient times—for example, just when you've settled into a new job, moved city, or thought you had everything figured out. Take my advice: When an opportunity presents itself, grab it with two hands and run with it as fast as you can.

I didn't expect to be offered an internship at one of the best design agencies in Europe when I had already spent almost 5,000 euros on a Master's degree. Years later, I didn't expect to be offered the opportunity to open a new agency in Los Angeles having literally just moved to New York from Europe. That's just the way opportunities happen. Roll with them.

OK, is your plan firmly affixed to your bedroom wall? Great, let's get started.

GETTING STARTED CHECKLIST*

- [ ] Complete the flowchart on page 12
- [ ] Write a statement of intent
- [ ] Make a list of steps to reach that goal
- [ ] Prioritize that list
- [ ] Focus on the top five things only
- [ ] Actually finish your portfolio website
- [ ] Write a resumé that doesn't suck
- [ ] Make a spreadsheet of your contacts
- [ ] Print a business card
- [ ] Buy some smart clothes
- [ ] Have a nice sleep

*Ignore this checklist at your peril!

FIGURE OUT WHAT YOU'RE REALLY GOOD AT

I once knew a very nice fellow—let's call him Roland Rocklicker—who wanted nothing more than to be a designer. At university, he would listen intently to every word from the professors, carefully filing away every typographic insight in his memory. He proudly sported a Helvetica T-shirt, drank coffee from a Pantone mug, subscribed to just about every design newsletter there was, and in all likelihood had a "Ban Comic Sans" tattoo on his buttocks. Late at night, he would silently repeat the names of fonts as he drifted into a sleep filled with dreams of winning a coveted D&AD Black Pencil design prize. Unfortunately for Roland, despite his hardest of tries, countless hours of practice, and best wishes, he was an absolutely terrible designer.

FIRST THINGS FIRST: SOME HARSH TRUTHS

Roland's tale of woe is a familiar one. All too often you, dear graduate, are misled at art or design school. You are made to believe that if you study photography you will become the next Annie Leibovitz. Focus on design, and you can be Jony Ive. Have an interest in hand-lettering—and occasionally like to pose nude—and you will become Stefan Sagmeister. And so on. When the bubble bursts and you realize that this will never happen, you are crushed. You settle for a second-place job, or perhaps even leave the industry.

Let's be clear: the purpose of telling you this truth is not to discourage you— the opposite, in fact. The key to a successful and fulfilling career is finding what you are actually good at as soon as humanly possible. Quite often, this isn't what you originally intended to do.

The key to a successful and fulfilling career is finding what you are actually good at as soon as humanly possible.

Over my career, I've seen that the people who do best are those who aren't afraid to shift direction: the visual designer whose true calling is actually brand strategy; the amateur photographer who is more skilled as a film producer; the writer who is brave enough to park their fantasy novel ambitions to pursue campaign writing—the list goes on.

Let's go back to beleaguered Roland for a second. As we have established, he was not cut out to be the next Jony Ive. However, as it turned out, he was a pretty amazing product manager*—a very sought-after role in the tech space. His deep knowledge of the technical aspects of design, combined with his practical sensibility, was a match made in heaven, and the last I heard he was very well off indeed.

* A product manager is the individual who leads the vision and development of a digital product or app.

IS THIS MY THING?

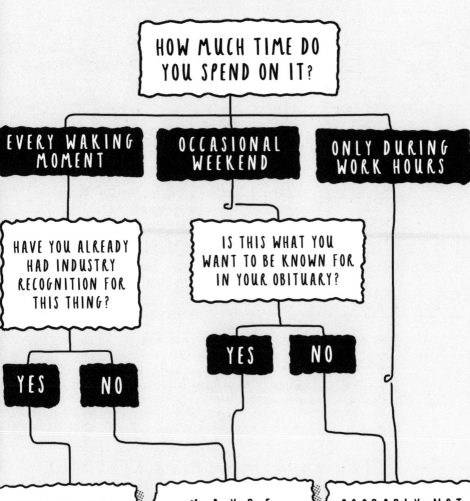

HOW MUCH TIME DO YOU SPEND ON IT?

EVERY WAKING MOMENT

OCCASIONAL WEEKEND

ONLY DURING WORK HOURS

HAVE YOU ALREADY HAD INDUSTRY RECOGNITION FOR THIS THING?

IS THIS WHAT YOU WANT TO BE KNOWN FOR IN YOUR OBITUARY?

YES **NO**

YES **NO**

YES, DO IT!

It sounds like you're already clear about your path and are on your way to get there. Don't give up!

MAYBE

Perhaps you haven't had enough experience to be sure. Look for a mentor to guide you or, if you have the luxury, think about further study.

PROBABLY NOT

It doesn't sound like you're passionate enough about this thing to invest the time required to really become a master.

FIND OUT WHAT YOU ARE GOOD AT

Let's be clear: Finding out what you're good at takes a considerable amount of tinkering around with many, many, many things that you aren't. You will not do this in one or two years. In fact, you'll be lucky to do it in ten. If you bought this book in the hope of revealing this over the course of reading, I'm afraid you're already too late for a refund.

EXPERIMENT WITH AS MUCH SHIT AS HUMANLY POSSIBLE

> Finding out what you're good at takes a considerable amount of tinkering around with many, many, many things that you aren't.

Early in your career, it is crucial to experiment with as many different styles, mediums, industries, and work environments as humanly possible. Learn something completely new. Try a fresh methodology. Use a different medium. Don't do the same thing twice. Creative experimentation (or "serious play," a term coined by the world-renowned designer Paula Scher in a 2008 TED talk[1]) is the path to growth. This is a process that never ends but continues throughout your career.

Bonus tip: The secret to staying creatively fresh is to continue creative play no matter how successful you become as your career progresses. Start a side hustle, build a personal project, write a book—it doesn't matter. Play is an ongoing part of your personal growth that doesn't stop until, quite frankly, you are pushing up the daisies. After all, if we lose the desire to learn, it's probably time to hightail it out of the creative industries. See more on serious play and side hustles on page 87.

OPEN YOURSELF UP TO FEEDBACK

All too often, junior creatives see criticism as negative. This is far from true. Instead, think of criticism as free advice. This is especially true in the early stages of your career, when you lack a point of reference for what is good and what isn't, and need to rely on the experience and guidance of others.

[1] https://www.ted.com/talks/paula_scher_great_design_is_serious_not_solemn

FIND A MENTOR

Early in my career, I was lucky enough to work with the famous designer (and general provocateur) Erik Spiekermann. Erik has a unique skill for instantly spotting where a person's natural talents lie. His outside perspective helped me sharpen my focus at a time when I didn't know whether I should be a designer, a filmmaker, an illustrator, or a writer. Spoiler alert: I'm still trying to decide.

Do the following: Gather a list of people who would be willing to act as mentors. This could include a trusted peer a few years ahead of you, a manager at your internship, or an ex-professor. Set up a review every six months. Open yourself up to their feedback—especially the negative parts. Take their input and make an action plan for how to improve and focus your personal development.

CONDUCT THE 10,000 HOURS TEST

The things that you will be truly great at almost always correlate directly with the things you love to do. Why is that? Well, it's simple: If you want to master just about anything—from world-domination techniques to horse-tail braiding—you need to throw yourself into it day and night, not just dabble at the weekends. Remember that old saying about it taking 10,000 hours to learn your craft? Yeah, that. And guess what, human nature dictates that you'll only spend 10,000 hours on something you really love. This is what I call the 10,000 hours test.

It's very easy: Ask yourself, "Am I willing to spend 10,000 hours on this to become a master at it?" It is a great way to test if you really love the thing, or just the idea of the thing. After all, in order to spend 10,000 hours on anything, you will need to develop an unhealthy obsession with this thing. You will read every book under the sun about the topic. You will shun birthdays, bar mitzvahs, funerals, and possibly even your own wedding to work on this thing. And you'll only do this—and become really good at it— if you are truly passionate about it.

Let me give you an example. My brother is a very successful fashion photographer, working in New York for brands such as *Vogue*, New York

CREATIVE PERSONALITY TYPES

The Visionary

The Artisan

The Organizer

The Detailer

The Pragmatist

The Entrepreneur

Fashion Week, and a host of others. He has loved cameras since he was a kid, obsessing day and night over taking photos. It was never work for him: He racked up his 10,000 hours pretty effortlessly and he naturally became great at it.

Experiment with new things and experiences, throw yourself into everything you do, fail a hundred times, and then a hundred times more.

On the other hand, I have always been a lousy photographer. My compositions are boring, my images are consistently overexposed, and the only time anyone comments positively on a photograph I have taken is when I include my adorable basset hound in it. I am a lousy photographer because, while I liked the idea of being a photographer, I've never loved it enough to dedicate myself day and night to perfecting the craft. I failed the 10,000 hours test because I was too busy obsessively drawing and writing as a kid, and—surprise, surprise—that's what I ended up doing.

CONSIDER FURTHER STUDY

If you're still finding yourself a bit lost, and you have the financial luxury of doing so, you should consider further study as a way to find your unique voice. A postgraduate course gives you the space to really explore what you love to do, and master your skills in that area. This book has some more details about this—see page 43.

BE PATIENT

Above all else, be patient. Discovering what you're good at takes a long time. Don't be afraid or too hard on yourself—experiment with new things and experiences, throw yourself into everything you do, fail a hundred times, and then a hundred times more. Find something you love to do, get obsessed and work bloody hard, and success will not be far behind. You'll be on the road to finding your own voice.

FINISH YOUR F*CKING PORTFOLIO

There will be no task in your life—hosting a successful dinner with your in-laws, getting a mortgage, or being acquitted in a murder trial—more difficult than creating your own portfolio. Except, of course, for the time when you create your *first* portfolio. This is an exercise in uncertainty, self-loathing, and even questioning one's right to exist.

THE PORTFOLIO CRISIS

Typically, the process of making your first portfolio looks something like this. You start out full of hopes and dreams—"I'm going to be the next Annie Leibovitz!," you proudly profess to your friends and colleagues, with aspirations of a portfolio that would impress even your most cretinous enemy.

Six months later, you are still working on the first page, after spending approximately nine hundred and fifty hours redesigning your logo twenty-seven times. You then move on to the images, redesigning each one approximately one hundred and twelve times. Feeling quite anxious by now, you shift gears and decide that it would be more sensible to write the copy for your case studies first. You proceed to do this, but by the time you complete the final case study three months later, you decide that they're not good enough after all, and that the only logical solution is to go back to the beginning and rewrite them one more time for good measure.

You despair, you wail, you cry for your mother, and yet the damn thing is still nowhere near finished.

Now in full panic mode, you try to shake the inertia by restarting the entire process from scratch. You despair, you wail, you cry for your mother, and yet the damn thing is still nowhere near finished. The whole thing comes to a head the night before your first interview, when, by some miracle, everything falls into place in a single all-nighter of sweat, tears, Red Bull, and a bout of inhuman mania akin to a rabid dog. And that, dear friend, is just the way it goes.

Now, far be it from me to lecture you on the process of creating your portfolio. However, allow me to share with you how to make a good one. Whether you want to do it over the course of six months or six hours is entirely up to you.

THE SIX STAGES OF THE PORTFOLIO CRISIS

1. Excitement

2. Confusion

3. Panic

4. Existential doubt

5. Mania

6. Completion

HOW TO CREATE A PORTFOLIO THAT DOESN'T SUCK

Several years ago, as I was preparing to leave Berlin for New York, I realized that my portfolio website needed a major overhaul. Years had passed without an update of any kind, and the site had become a sprawling hodgepodge of garbage without a purpose, theme, or unique voice. Almost daily, I was getting the very worst kind of freelance offers and freebie requests such as "Can you please design a logo in Microsoft Word for my dog?"

At that time, I was design director at a big agency in Europe and was regularly publishing articles in industry magazines. Quite frankly, it was beyond a joke that my website still showed mostly student projects and had not been updated in a very, very, very long time. Entering full panic mode because I had job interviews in New York looming, I embarked on a laser-focussed refresh of my personal brand and portfolio that I ended up completing in a single weekend. It was the best portfolio I ever had, and for one simple reason: I approached it as if it were a commercial client project. Here's how:

STEP ONE: DEFINE A CLEAR PURPOSE AND STRATEGY

This is the most important part of the process. Before you take another breath, ask yourself two questions.

The first question to ask is, "What do I want to get out of this?" Do you want to get more freelance work? Are you looking for a new job, and if so, where? Or perhaps you don't care and simply want to make a statement that says, "I exist."

The second question to ask is, "Who is the end user?" Is it a potential employer, an art gallery, a design publication, or your own mother?

Understanding these two questions is key to the success of your portfolio. Do not proceed to the next step unless you are crystal clear on the answers to both.

HOW SHOULD I PRESENT MY WORK?

WHAT IS YOUR GOAL?

FIND A JOB   **ATTRACT CLIENTS**   **SELL SOMETHING**

HOW IS YOUR WORK BEST REPRESENTED?

HOW MANY YEARS OF WORK EXPERIENCE DO YOU HAVE?

IT NEEDS EXPLANATION   **PRIMARILY VISUAL WORK**

LESS THAN THREE   **MORE THAN THREE**

WEBSITE WITH PERSONAL WORK

Chances are that your role on commercial projects is minimal at this stage. Show your skills with personal projects that you've worked on end to end, from concept to execution.

WEBSITE WITH COMMERCIAL WORK

Showing commercial work early in your career is a tricky business, but if you have it, flaunt it. It's the best way to convince a potential employer or client that you're a safe choice.

AN AWESOME SOCIAL PRESENCE

Grow your following by going where your audience is. Especially important for promoting highly visual skills like illustration or photography, or selling prints, art, etc.

STEP TWO: FIGURE OUT WHAT IS UNIQUE ABOUT YOU, AND OWN IT

As with any self-branding exercise, fully understanding what makes you unique is key. Are you the sophisticated minimalist? Or the zany maximalist who specializes in eye-popping patterns and neon colors? Even if you know exactly what you do, how you do it is even more important.

> As with any self-branding exercise, fully understanding what makes you unique is key.

To be clear, this is easier said than done. A piece of advice: Don't get stuck in your own head. It's often a good idea to ask a group of peers to describe the one thing that stands out about your work. Don't take it verbatim, but getting an outside opinion will help you get unstuck.

I asked myself this question early in the process. I realized that, for better or worse, people always comment that I swear a lot and am occasionally funny. Another quirk of mine is that every morning I write a daily to-do list with a thick Pentel Sign pen. "Swearing and thick hand-lettering?" I thought. "I can own this." This became a core part of my personal brand and still is to this day.

STEP THREE: INCLUDE ONLY THE TYPE OF WORK YOU WANT TO DO MORE OF

If you don't want to do more of a certain type of work, don't include it in your portfolio. You must resist the urge, no matter how good the work is, how many awards it has won, or how much your mom says she loves it. Before you include a piece of work in your book, you must first ask yourself: "Is this in line with the work I want to do in the future?"

For example, in the past you may have prided yourself on being a generalist doing a mixture of illustration, design, and photography, but now you want to move into fashion photography. It is a no-brainer: show only fashion photography in your portfolio, write about fashion photography, and position yourself as an expert on fashion photography.

> If you don't want to do more of a certain type of work, don't include it in your portfolio.

When I was moving to New York, I wanted to shift from design into art direction. With ideas of Madison Avenue at the forefront of my mind, I wanted to try out the ad world. With that in mind, I said "Auf wiedersehen" to the smattering of minimalist Josef Müller-Brockmann grids and Swiss typography that were in the back pages of my portfolio.

THE DOS & DON'TS OF YOUR PORTFOLIO WEBSITE

DO...

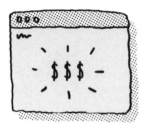

Invest some $$$ in a good platform

Be laser-focussed on what you include

Actually launch the damn thing

DON'T...

Spend three years trying to build it yourself

Cram in as much crap as humanly possible

Noodle over it for an eternity

STEP FOUR: EDIT, EDIT, EDIT, AND THEN EDIT SOME MORE

The real secret to turning your new-found focus into a great portfolio is the editing process. Everything that doesn't match your positioning must be removed.

But what happens, I hear you cry, if you don't have any work in your "new" direction? Maybe your portfolio is full of potato printing when you really want to be a logo designer. The secret: Make it up. Take a brand you love and redesign their logo. Find a real brief online and then add your own take on it. Approach it like a real project—write a brief, set yourself a problem to solve, then make a killer case study out of it. Document the process in detail, and be open that this was a self-initiated brief. No employer who is looking at your portfolio cares. In truth, half the stuff in people's portfolios is made up, anyway.

A good trick to avoid procrastinating over meaningless details is to publicly announce a launch date.

STEP FIVE: LAUNCH THE DAMN THING

We've all been there: "It's not ready yet—just a bit more polishing." Bullshit. When it comes to launching your website, I can't stress this enough: Launch the damn thing, even if it's not finished. You can polish the final details for all eternity.

A good trick to avoid procrastinating over meaningless details is to publicly announce a launch date. Communicate this date as widely as possible to your friends, enemies, and followers. This means you have to stick to it or risk enduring side effects that include (but are not limited to) public shaming, disgrace, ridicule, anxiety, insomnia, constipation, hair loss, insanity, or total loss of bowel function.

COMMERCIAL WORK
AND YOUR PORTFOLIO

A note on including commercial work in your portfolio. For recent graduates and juniors, this can be a tricky topic. We've all been there—it's your first job and you've just landed yourself a dream project for an awesome brand. As a junior, you may play a minor role, perhaps just updating some copy or reapplying existing design styles to a layout.

Months later, the time comes to update your portfolio for a new job and you ask yourself if you should include that project. Surely any type of work on a project means you have earned the right to put it in your portfolio? While technically the answer may be yes, there are a couple of reasons why you shouldn't include these types of project in your book.

YOU WILL GET FOUND OUT (TRUST ME)
As a creative director whose job it is to look at the portfolios of potential designers, I frequently see the same project appear again and again in different people's books. While each person may indeed have worked on it to some extent, often their respective role was simply editing four pixels of an existing design, dropping in some new copy, or some other very minor role. This overlap does not reflect well on anybody who worked on the project, and it is very easy for a potential employer to get to the bottom of who the real creative lead was.

YOU'RE HIDING YOUR REAL TALENT
The bigger problem with including this kind of work is the skills that you are not showing. Essentially, you're featuring someone else's work instead of highlighting your own creative and problem-solving skills. It just does not make sense.

WHAT I PUT IN MY PORTFOLIO

My guideline on what to include in my portfolio is whether or not I took a leading role in the creative direction of the project. I ask myself:

• Was I involved in coming up with the actual creative idea?
• Did I have a key role in the direction or execution?
• Am I able to state clearly my role and have I credited the rest of the team?

"But I still want people to know I've worked with big clients!" I hear you say. And of course you should. But rather than including the work itself, think about creating a section on your site or CV where you simply list the clients you've worked for.

For example, I worked on several projects for big brands when I was in New York. While I am proud of this work, it does not clearly demonstrate my personal skills because it was undertaken as part of a much larger team. Instead of adding the projects on my website or portfolio, I include a list of the brands that I have worked with on my 'About/Clients' page and in my bio.

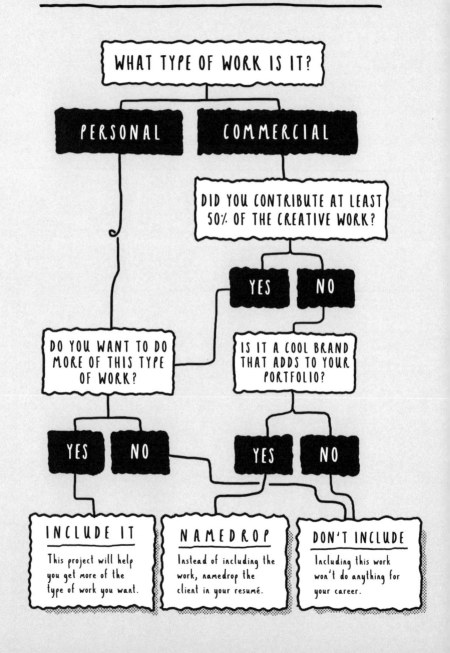

SMALLER PROJECTS ARE BETTER FOR YOUR PORTFOLIO

Even when you do play a significant role in a large project, in many cases there are simply too many people involved to give a sense of an individual's personality or creative style when it is included in a portfolio. In short: Your own creative voice gets lost. For that reason, it is this author's opinion that creatives should limit the number of big commercial projects in their portfolio.

When I'm reviewing portfolios, I always get a much better sense of a creative's skills and interests from personal and smaller projects. This type of work gives a potential employer a better understanding of who they are and whether or not they are the right fit for a prospective project. For example, my personal project *Adloids* (a satirical news publication on the advertising industry) will give a potential colleague a much better sense of who I am as an art director than a banner ad that I created for a bank with a team of over twenty people.

> When I'm reviewing portfolios, I always get a much better sense of a creative's skills and interests from personal and smaller projects.

Good work is about using your brain. Forget the lure of including big commercial projects and brands in your portfolio; be selective about how you show off your skills instead. Smart ideas beat big names every time. And it doesn't take a million bucks to show that.

CONSIDER FURTHER STUDY

There are some who say that an undergraduate degree—let alone a postgraduate degree—is not necessary in order to have a successful creative career. This is certainly true. After all, some of the most successful individuals in the world, from Michael Kors to Frida Kahlo, did not attend university. Furthermore, some of the most notable innovators (Steve Jobs being the obvious poster boy for this) dropped out of university without a backward glance.

However, not everyone is born with the single-minded vision to create the next iPod or paint the modern-day *The Two Fridas*. For the majority of us, finding one's way takes time, experimentation, and lots of failure. Enter the postgraduate degree: an option for those who need to create a space to find their creative voice.

WHEN DOES FURTHER STUDY MAKE SENSE?

Doing a postgraduate degree is a big commitment, and you need to be sure that it will deliver tangible, long-term value for your career.

First things first: postgraduate study isn't for everyone. For starters, it is expensive. In London, where I completed my postgrad, an average two-year Master's degree can cost around £7,000[2]. In the US, where my wife studied, the cost is significantly more—anywhere between $30,000 and $120,000[3] is considered acceptable (but, if you ask me, this is about as acceptable as smoking on airplanes or chewing gum with your mouth open). And then there is the longer and much more expensive doctorate. However you look at it, doing a postgraduate degree is a big commitment, and you need to be sure that it will deliver tangible, long-term value for your career.

Here are some occasions when continued study might make sense:

YOU'RE STRUGGLING TO FIND YOUR OWN "STYLE"
For those who argue that a postgraduate degree is just for those with a penchant for the academic, think again. A postgraduate degree can act as a reset button in your career when it comes to defining your own creative voice. It is a moment when you say, "I'm serious about finding what makes my work unique" and carve out a year (or more) of your life to do just that.

This is especially true of the creative careers that involve a lot of personal expression—fashion photography, illustration, filmmaking, and the like. Finding your own style in this type of field involves significant exploration, and sometimes that isn't possible on the side of a full-time job. A postgraduate degree will give you the space and the mentorship to—at the risk of sounding like a cheap self-help salesperson—"find yourself."

When I graduated from my undergraduate degree, I was torn between a career in design and one in illustration (I studied both as an undergraduate). During my Master's degree in London, the biggest self-learning was figuring out how I could combine these two fields into a unique creative style that I still use to this day.

[2] https://www.findamasters.com/funding/guides/cost-of-a-masters.aspx
[3] https://www.bestmastersdegrees.com/best-masters-degrees-faq/how-much-does-a-masters-degree-cost

IS FURTHER STUDY FOR ME?

WHAT IS YOUR END GOAL

START A BUSINESS

BECOME AN EDUCATOR

GET A JOB

ARE YOU CLEAR ON YOUR VALUE PROP AND DO YOU HAVE SOME BUSINESS BASICS?

DO YOU ALREADY HAVE A GOOD PORTFOLIO AND SOME EXPERIENCE?

NO **YES**

NO **YES**

YES, PROBABLY

Further study can be a great way to find your unique creative voice or learn new business skills.

MAYBE

A postgrad is a good way to build your portfolio. For educators, keep in mind that some real experience is recommended first.

PROBABLY NOT

A postgrad won't significantly increase your chances of landing a job unless you want to change direction.

YOU'RE LOOKING FOR AN ALTERNATIVE WAY TO START A CAREER ABROAD

Another viable reason for further study is for those looking to start a career abroad, but who have little work experience, a less-than-perfect portfolio, and/or few contacts in their desired location. Studying abroad can be a way to get your career started in a new city or country, allowing you to build your network of contacts, familiarize yourself with the local creative scene, and build up a locally relevant portfolio.

YOU'RE THINKING ABOUT STARTING YOUR OWN BUSINESS

By and large, business basics in creative education is still a fringe subject that is not taught in nearly enough detail in undergraduate courses (hence this author writing this book). Even if you're not doing an MBA, most postgraduate courses cover the business side of the creative industries in significantly more detail than your undergraduate program. If learning more about the business side is important for you, a postgraduate degree is definitely worth considering.

YOU KNOW YOU MIGHT NEED A VISA IN A FEW YEARS

While a postgraduate degree is by no means necessary for a visa, it doesn't hurt. It is an indisputable fact that if you have a qualification on your resumé, it will make it easier to get a work visa. For several visa categories, a university qualification is a must-have, and even the ones that don't absolutely require it will be influenced by the perception that this person is qualified in their craft "on paper."

HOW TO PICK THE RIGHT COURSE

You've decided to do a postgraduate course, and right now are probably staring at a pile of prospectuses that are covering the entire surface area of your dining table, each one squealing "Pick me!" Before you spin into an indecisive state of hyperventilation, take a moment and read through the following checklist:

BE CLEAR ON WHY YOU'RE DOING IT

The first and most important step to finding the right course (and succeeding at it) is to ask yourself, "Why am I doing this and what do I want to get out of it?" Perhaps you want to find your unique style. Perhaps you want to grow your portfolio in a specific area. Or maybe you want to move away from practice entirely, and shift your career towards a more academic focus. Being clear about this goal before you even open a prospectus is critical. Not sure what this should be? Look at your "statement of intent" back on page 15. If doing a postgraduate degree doesn't match with your overall statement of intent, it probably isn't a good idea.

DECIDE ON PART-TIME VS. FULL TIME

Many postgraduate courses offer both full-time and part-time options. In this author's opinion, when it comes to creative postgraduate degrees— especially practical ones—full-time is the marginally better approach because you will fully immerse yourself for a dedicated period of time. However, part-time has the advantage that you don't give up your day job, and it allows you to spread the cost of your degree over time. There are quite a few designers I've worked with who have done postgraduate degrees in their spare time with no ill effects to either their job or their education. It comes down to how well you juggle multiple things.

DO YOUR RESEARCH

One would think this is a glaringly obvious point; however, it is surprising the number of people I've spoken to about their Master's degree who say "It wasn't what I expected." Eliminate the element of surprise by being thorough in your research into the course, what is covered, what isn't, who will be tutoring you, and what the alumni are doing now.

VISIT THE CAMPUS

While Google Street View is a remarkable piece of technology, actually visiting the campus in person is crucial if you are to get a sense of the university. When I was researching my Master's, I applied to a few courses that were, on paper, all fine choices. The most prestigious one—which shall remain nameless for fear of a lawsuit—was the one my peers insisted was the right choice. Taking my own advice, I visited their campus in London, where it was immediately clear that the most prestigious choice was also the most pretentious. Having no desire to pick up the mannerisms of an English toff, I struck this university from my list and never looked back.

MEET THE LECTURERS

Do not skip this step under any circumstances. You are about to spend a shitload of money on the mentorship of these lecturers, so you must take the time to meet all of them. No matter how good a reputation a postgraduate course has, if you don't gel with the lecturers, it is the wrong choice for you.

No matter how good a reputation a postgraduate course has, if you don't gel with the lecturers, it is the wrong choice for you.

POSTGRADUATE MYTHS

TRUE

Discover your unique
creative voice

Work autonomously
and set your schedule

Be expected to act
like an adult

FALSE

Have a guaranteed path
to landing a job

Get a detailed list
of what to do

Party like
it's 2001

SPEAK TO PAST STUDENTS

Most universities worth their salt will have no problem connecting you with graduates. Ask them about their experience on the course, what did and didn't work well, and, most importantly, what they are doing now. After all, if ninety percent of them are currently working in McDonald's, it's probably not the right course for you unless your goal is to lead the way in the glorious world of fast food.

MASTER'S OR DOCTORATE?

When it comes to postgraduate study, a common question from potential students is what the benefits are of a Master's versus a doctorate. In truth, if you are doing a postgraduate with a view to improving your creative practice (for example, if you wish to open a creative business, become a practicing creative, etc.), it is this author's opinion that a Master's is as far as you should go.

On the other hand, if you have a desire to go down a more academic path—such as critical writing, research, or lecturing—a doctorate may be the right path for you. Also, having a PhD has the added benefit that you can publicly correct people who do not use the title "Doctor" when they address you. Better still, you can proudly give a resounding "Yes" if a flight attendant asks "Is there a doctor on board?" What's not to love about that?

MAKING THE MOST OF THE POSTGRADUATE DEGREE

Once you've decided on the course, the only thing left is to actually do it. Regardless of whether you're newly graduated or going back to school after a few years of working, if this is your first postgraduate degree, you should prepare for a very different experience from your undergrad.

The amount of self-motivation required for a postgraduate degree throws a lot of people.

BE PREPARED TO BE (MOSTLY) AUTONOMOUS

The amount of self-motivation required for a postgraduate degree throws a lot of people. In stark contrast to your undergraduate degree, where you are namby-pambied like a petulant child by your professors, in a postgraduate degree you will largely set your own briefs, timelines, and overall area of focus. In many ways, you are on your own. Your professors are more like mentors to whom you turn for occasional support than teachers who provide a clear path.

IT IS WHAT YOU MAKE OF IT

This may seem an obvious statement for any of life's undertakings, but it is especially true when it comes to postgraduate study. To succeed, you must get into a mindset where you are in the driving seat. This is true regardless of the subject, curriculum, or who your tutors are. You set the schedule, the topics, and the outcomes. Much like the real world, you are the master of your destiny.

EXPECT TO PARTY LESS

When it comes to social activity, postgraduate life is about as far as you can get from that of an undergrad (which, I'll admit, I was more than a little disappointed about). Compared to an undergraduate degree where your classmates are full-time for three or four years, postgraduate life is a mix of people with full-time jobs, a little older, and, in general, more serious about their careers. Expect less beer pong, fewer frat parties, and more actual work. Sorry.

YOU NEED TO GET SERIOUS ABOUT YOUR PERSONAL BRAND

A postgraduate study is the ideal time to re-audit and professionalize your personal brand in light of your new direction. Review your portfolio and professional social media accounts. Are they in line with the new style of work, direction, or career goals you've discovered during your further studies? If not, now is the time to fix it before you get sucked back into the real world. Finally, for those of you still mentally stuck at age 18, it's time to finally bid farewell to your personal social media accounts that are filled with photos of you vomiting over the floor of a frat house. Or at least make them private.

> It's time to finally bid farewell to your personal social media accounts filled with photos of you vomiting

THE POSTGRADUATE CHECKLIST

- [ ] Be clear about why you're doing it
- [ ] Assess the syllabus against your goal
- [ ] Weigh up costs vs return
- [ ] Visit the campus in person
- [ ] Speak with all the professors in advance
- [ ] Stalk former students on LinkedIn to check what they are actually doing
- [ ] Buy a nice bag to look cool
- [ ] Cancel your social plans
- [ ] Be ready to network like a MoFo
- [ ] Don't panic when you see your friends in jobs while you're still in school. It'll be worth it in the long run*

*Assuming you completed this amazing checklist

DO AN INTERNSHIP (OR TWO)

Take my advice: Do an internship. Do two. Maybe even three. When you are fresh out of university, the truth is that no matter how good your portfolio, how many student awards you have won, or how smitten your professors were with your digital paintings of your cat Thomas, you are almost certainly underqualified for most full-time jobs simply because of your lack of real-world experience. An internship will sneak you into that great company that you wouldn't have a chance of getting into otherwise.

So, how do you go about getting an internship at a killer studio, should you expect it to be paid, and, perhaps most importantly, how do you turn it into a full-time position? Read on.

INTERNSHIPS IN THE CREATIVE INDUSTRIES

Most creative companies worth their salt have an internship program of some kind. For people in the early stages of a career who naturally don't have a ton of experience, an internship can be one of the best routes into a great studio that may not hire you immediately. In most studios, the best interns are usually on an automatic path to a full-time gig. For example, at almost all the design agencies I know, a significant number of senior employees started their careers as interns at the company—myself included.

An internship can be one of the best routes into a great studio that may not hire you immediately.

For me, it started with an unexpected phone call from a long, unfamiliar number some time in 2010. A curious accent greeted me on the other end of the line: "Hallo, ezz diss Herr Vudds?" It was over a month since I had sent a tranche of applications to agencies that I was, quite frankly, grossly underqualified for, so I had zero expectations of getting a response, let alone a phone call.

As it transpired, it was not an ex-Governor of California, or a long-lost Uncle Herkenhoff calling to inform me of a vast inheritance, but an offer of an internship at a prestigious design agency in Berlin. Woefully unprepared, not speaking a word of German—and, perhaps most worryingly, never having lived away from my mom's house—I packed a small bag and made the trip to a land of sausages, lack of humor, and a history of walls.

Over the course of three months, I was thrown in at the deep end, starting out on simple tasks such as packaging mockups of new logos and retouching photos, moving on to helping out on small design tasks, and ultimately working my way up to designing the visual identity on a global campaign for a well-known energy drinks brand of the bovine variety. Most importantly, I was given a mentor who nudged me in the right direction. At night I would sit on the banks of the River Spree drinking ridiculously underpriced Berliner Pilsner with our team. It was an awesome time in my career. When I finished my internship, I was offered a freelance position, which turned into a full-time position, which turned into Design Director, Creative Director, followed by Chief Creative Officer, before ultimately working my way into the role of CEO of the US offices.

INTERN MYTHS: TRUE OR FALSE

1

Your main job is the walking of the office dog

2

You will have to run your own projects

3

You should expect to get paid a fair wage

4

You are the maker of the creative director's coffee

5

Long hours and weekend work are part of it

6

You'll do a fair share of menial tasks

ANSWERS: 1=F, 2=T, 3=F, 4=T, 5=T, 6=T

Take this advice to heart: Even with the greatest portfolio in the world, your chances of getting hired full-time at a studio right out of university—especially a good one—without any experience are relatively low. Furthermore, it is this author's opinion that the majority of junior creatives should not waste their time looking for a full-time job immediately anyway. Now is the time to learn, to fuck up, to experiment.

When you do prove yourself as an intern, a conversion to a junior position is much more likely than when you apply anonymously through the HR department.

While an internship means that you start off at the bottom of the pecking order, it also means significantly more leeway when you inevitably mess something up, and you will always have the underdog card and the ability to surprise. Again, when you do prove yourself as an intern, a conversion to a junior position is much more likely than when you apply anonymously through the HR department.

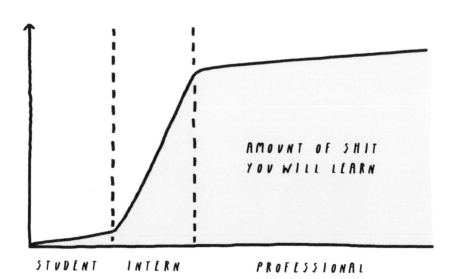

AMOUNT OF SHIT
YOU WILL LEARN

STUDENT   INTERN   PROFESSIONAL

APPLYING FOR INTERNSHIPS

The first time you apply for a role of any kind—from an internship to a full-time job—is a daunting undertaking. After all, it's your first time putting yourself and your work out there for judgment in front of a stranger. Here are some things to keep in mind when applying for that first internship:

ONLY APPLY TO PLACES YOU REALLY LOVE
This is the number one rule of applying for internships: Only apply to places that you really want to work at: The amazing agency in New York that you dreamed about, the studio in Los Angeles that produced your favorite TV show, the tech startup in Silicon Valley that you believe will change the world. Now is not the time to be humble—there is zero purpose in doing an internship at the local agency in your small town that is mediocre at best. Aim high. Remember, an internship is your back door into a company that you wouldn't have a chance of getting into otherwise.

WORK YOUR UNIVERSITY CONTACTS
Most universities have an internship program of sorts. If yours does, be sure to apply for it. The downside is that everyone in your class will apply for that one position too. Broaden your network and your options by proactively making contact with visiting lecturers. Approach them after their talk, follow up with them, meet them for coffee, share your work with them—in short, make a connection and bug the shit out of them until you get a meeting. As the old saying goes, the squeaky wheel gets the oil.

DO MORE THAN ONE INTERNSHIP (BUT KEEP IT UNDER THREE)
Early in your career, you will need to gather as much real-world experience as possible. Don't be afraid to extend an internship if you're learning a lot, and even consider doing a second one if the first doesn't result in a job. However, limit the number of internships on your resumé to three. More than this can be seen as a red flag for a potential employer, who may question why none of these internships resulted in a job offer.

DON'T BE AFRAID OF A COLD INTERNSHIP SEARCH
While getting an internship through a school program or existing contacts is all well and good, the vast majority of you will probably be searching for an internship cold—that is, reaching out to companies that have never heard of you. For more details about how to do this, skip ahead to the How Find a job you love section on page 63.

INTERN SURVIVAL KIT

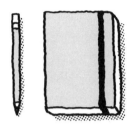

Pen and paper for
actually taking notes

Feedback

An open ear for
listening to feedback

Time-keeping device for
not missing deadlines

Groogle

The internet to find all
the shit you don't know

A camera to capture
behind-the-scenes work

A taste for caffeine
of any variety

WHAT YOU SHOULD EXPECT AS AN INTERN

There are a lot of misconceptions when it comes to what to expect. Will I be the person making the coffee for the creative director? Should I be the office dog walker? Will I have a mentor? Should an internship be paid? Truthfully, the creative industries have benefited from the less-than-informed interns who are willing to work for free and get little in terms of mentorship or learning opportunities in return.

Remember this, my would-be intern: For what you lack in real-world skills, as an intern, you bring a huge amount of value and energy to a studio. For example, at our agency, the interns bring a fresh energy to our culture that simply doesn't come with a more seasoned creative. When it comes to ideation, an intern's lack of experience can be a significant strength, as they often provide a totally left-field approach to a brief. In short, internships are not a one-sided value-add for the intern. When managed well, interns bring significant value to any creative workplace.

> An intern's lack of experience can be a significant strength, as they often provide a totally left-field approach to a brief.

With that in mind, here are the things that you should expect from any internship placement, and a few others that the team will expect from you:

EXPECT TO WORK FASTER THAN YOU EVER HAVE BEFORE

The biggest difference between university and the real world is the pace at which you work. I promise you, although the months in advance of your graduate show seemed hectic and fast-paced, they are nothing—nothing—compared with the speed at which you will need to work in the real world. At university you have weeks, sometimes months, to complete a task. In the real world it may be days or even hours. When an intern starts at our agency, this is always the biggest shock, and the thing they struggle with most. Remember, in the words of Facebook COO Sheryl Sandberg, Done is better than perfect.

BE ABLE TO MANAGE YOUR TIME

The most frequent reason why we don't convert an otherwise talented intern to a full-time employee comes down to one failing: Bad time management. All too often, interns treat deadlines as fluid entities that can shift with the "ready-ness" of a piece of work. Keep this in mind: Missing a deadline once is forgivable. Twice is a red flag. More than twice and you're out.

> The biggest difference between university and the real world is the pace at which you work.

The solution to better time management when it comes to creative projects is simple: Before you start a project, break it down into several work packages, and plan each one on a timeline. For example, a logo design project will consist of several stages: Initial ideation, pencil sketches, digitizing the artwork, creating a presentation, working in internal feedback, and finally presenting to the client. Timebox each step of the process in advance and keep each one in its "box."

HAVE A MENTOR

Every intern needs a mentor. The role of your mentor is to provide advice, help identify your strengths and weaknesses, provide wisdom when things are shitty, and generally guide you along the way. Any internship program worth its salt will match you with a mentor on your first day. If you aren't assigned a mentor when you start, be sure to ask.

BE PREPARED TO DO GRUNT WORK...

As an intern, you can expect a fair dose of image searching, preparing boards, doing mockups for presentations, and even tasks like proofreading. The best interns—and the ones we make a point of converting to full-time employees—are the ones who treat every task, no matter how small, as their moment to shine.

...BUT REMEMBER YOU'RE NOT THERE TO MAKE THE COFFEE

Remember, as an intern you are there to learn. If you are only being assigned menial tasks that have no learning value for your actual career trajectory— walking the office dog, picking up the creative director's coffee—take it as a major red flag. Politely contact your mentor or someone in HR to discuss the matter.

GET PAID

Last, but certainly not least, is the prickly topic of payment. It is this author's opinion that all internships should be paid. As a general guideline, you can expect minimum wage. Sometimes this is made up in part with benefits such as a travel allowance or a metrocard.

If an internship is unpaid, it is an immediate red flag that the company doesn't take placements seriously. A lack of payment often indicates a less structured program, lack of a mentor, and a lot of grunt work.

GOING FROM INTERNSHIP TO FULL—TIME POSITION

There comes a time when all internships come to an end. Then, of course, the big question is how to turn an internship into a full-time gig. The answer is simple: In whatever time you have as an intern, and whatever tasks you are given, you must go above and beyond every time. When you are asked to do a quick mockup of a website for a pitch, figure out how to build it in code and animate it. If you're an assistant on a photoshoot, produce a behind-the-scenes video for the photographer. If you are asked to walk the office dog, take it on the best damned walk that dog has ever experienced in its little canine life.

In whatever time you have as an intern, and whatever tasks you are given, you must go above and beyond every time.

If you're not offered a job right away, don't panic. As you'll see in the next chapter, the secret to landing a job in the best studio in the business has very little to do with having the best portfolio, but rather, having the best connection with the people working there. Your internship has given you months to build that connection. Once you finish the placement, all you have to do is maintain regular meetups with the team, share updates on your latest work, and drop the occasional email with a smattering of praise for the creative director's new project. Time will take care of the rest.

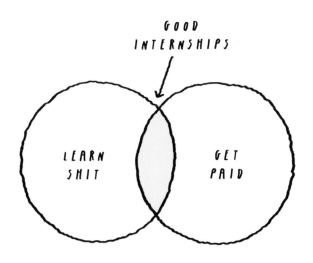

GOOD
INTERNSHIPS

LEARN
SHIT

GET
PAID

FIND A JOB YOU LOVE

Admit it: You skipped to this chapter first. In fact, you're probably still lurking in the book store right now, trying to glean an insight or two before a spotty clerk tells you to buy the book or move along. Either way, the "secret" to finding a job is probably one of the first questions you'll ask as a young creative. Well, if you are looking for the single most important insight about finding a job you love in the creative industries before you put this book back on the shelf, here it is: It's not about having the best portfolio. In fact, it's not about having the second-best, or even the third-best portfolio for that matter. The real truth is that it is about being the most *persistent*. And being bloody organized.

YOUR FIRST JOB HUNT

The first proactive job search of my life came when I was four years into my career—probably later than it does for most. I had spent almost four years working in Berlin as a design director at a big agency. Until that point, I had the good fortune to have gone from opportunity to opportunity—freelancing in London, then an internship in Berlin, then being promoted from internship to designer to design director. But, as with all jobs, no matter how good, eventually the time came to do something completely different. The location of choice: New York.

At the time, I had zero contacts, reputation, or experience in New York. Perhaps most worrying was the fact that I had never even visited the city in my entire life. Nonetheless, I was consumed by an overwhelming desire to live there—inspired by an adolescence spent watching *Friends* and *Seinfeld*, and an unhealthy obsession with good pizza. And so, in August 2014, I found myself starting the first proper job hunt of my career.

HOW TO FIND A JOB YOU LOVE

For the purposes of this chapter, we will assume that you are starting a job search relatively cold. By "cold," I do not mean a job search accompanied by a chilled beer. Rather, I mean that you are reaching out to people or companies that you do not know. Searching for a job cold is always tough, but it is not impossible, as some would have you believe. In reality it's simply about doing your research and being prepared and knowledgeable about who you're dealing with.

Before you are tempted to dive in and send your first email, complete the following steps:

STEP ONE: BE PREPARED
There is nothing worse than landing a spontaneous meeting with a famous creative director and then having no portfolio, website, or even business card to show them. Your first task will be to complete the checklist over the page. Do not proceed until all items are complete.

JOB HUNTING DOS & DON'TS

DO ...

DON'T ...

Be prepared before
you start applying

Email blast 743
companies at once

Research the shit out of
everywhere you apply to

Send giant PDF files to
the creative director

Contact the creative
director directly

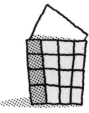

Send generic cover letters
with your applications

JOB PREP CHECKLIST

- [ ] Portfolio website live
- [ ] Resumé updated and printed
- [ ] Business card printed
- [ ] LinkedIn page up-to-date
- [ ] Spreadsheet of contacts
- [ ] Shortlist of companies
- [ ] Research file on these companies
- [ ] Personalized cover letters prepared
- [ ] Clothes actually washed
- [ ] Social media accounts scrubbed of all embarrassing or incriminating events. Perhaps it's easier to just delete them

Completed the above? Time to bug some creative directors!

STEP TWO: MAKE A PROPER CONTACTS LIST

Sound boring? It is. But a well-maintained contacts list is something that you will come back to again and again throughout your career. A Google spreadsheet is a good format for this. Include contact details, website, etc. Be sure to revisit this list regularly (even when you have a job), so it is always up-to-date when you need it. This list should have at least fifty entries.

A well-maintained contacts list is something that you will come back to again and again throughout your career.

STEP THREE: PRIORITIZE AND EDIT

Any idiot can get a job—that's not the title of this chapter. You want to find a job you love. Finding a job you love starts with the contents of your contacts list. It's as simple as this: garbage in, garbage out. If you eliminate all places that you don't want to work from the list, you'll never have to work there. Your edited list should have at least twenty entries. Now prioritize the list, because the next step requires significant time investment on each one.

STEP FOUR: RESEARCH, RESEARCH, AND MORE RESEARCH

This is the hard part. For every possible place you are thinking of applying, you need to play the role of a private detective and dive deep into every little detail about this company: How long have they been around? What is their manifesto? What is their latest project, and did it win awards? How is the company structured? What methodology do they use? Who are the creative leaders? Who would you report to directly? What is that person's background? What sort of work do they love to do? What is the name of their pet goldfish? You get the idea.

INSIDER TIPS ON JOB APPLICATIONS

By now, you should have enough data on the company to make Mark Zuckerberg jealous. Let's put this to good use on your first job application.

First, a word of advice from someone who reviews creative applicants almost daily: You have approximately five seconds to make an impression with your job application. Don't believe me? Allow me to give you some context from a creative director's perspective.

You have approximately five seconds to make an impression with your job application.

The hiring process usually starts with a cheery note from a project manager informing me that we need to hire a new team member. This email immediately adds a gloomy layer to the day. The feeling is similar to when my wife informs me when it is that time of the year that I must forage through every hardware store in California to procure the perfect Christmas tree. Now, don't get me wrong—I thoroughly enjoy interviewing people—but the thought of spending hours upon hours each week trawling through our clunky HR software (and let's be honest—all HR software is clunky) reviewing hundreds, if not thousands, of applicants fills me with dread.

To give you, dear reader, a sense of the numbers that a creative director will need to review for any single role, every creative position we post on our website gets between 100 and 300 applications per week. This translates to between 20 and 60 applications per day that someone (usually me) must review, depending on how diligent the pre-screening is.

Now, keep in mind that I run a relatively small creative agency, so consider these numbers very conservative. At a larger agency, the numbers are infinitely bigger. Even when you factor in an HR department that generally weeds out the first round of unsuitable candidates, the fact remains: If your portfolio actually makes it in front of the creative director, you have an incredibly short amount of time in which to impress.

With that in mind, here are a few things to help you stand out from the rest of the pack (unless, of course, they have shared in your infinite wisdom to purchase this book):

CONTACT THE COMPANY BEFORE THEY HAVE AN OPEN POSITION

Reaching out to a creative company before they even have an open position is one of the most effective tactics for getting ahead of the pack. If you do this, you get to speak with the company before they are flooded with applicants for a role. Most importantly, you demonstrate a genuine interest in their company, and increase the odds of being at the forefront of their mind when a position does open up. Always frame your correspondence in a knowledgeable manner, such as "I understand you're not hiring now, but I would love to drop by and hear about the work you're doing on such and such a project."

> Reaching out to a creative company before they even have an open position is one of the most effective tactics for getting ahead of the pack.

REACH OUT TO THE CREATIVE DIRECTOR DIRECTLY

Always contact the creative director first. I would estimate that at least 75 percent of successful job applicants have reached out to me directly. Learn something about them; flatter them with your knowledge of an obscure project from their past career. Ask if you can meet them for a ten-minute coffee. Pick up a copy of their latest book. 99.9 percent of creative directors are egomaniacs and will succumb to flattery of any kind. Unless your work is absolute garbage, if you make a direct personal connection with the creative director, you will almost certainly make it through to a second-round interview. Combine this with tip number one and you are guaranteed to be at least one step ahead.

DON'T COPY AND PASTE YOUR COVER LETTER ...

Copy-and-pasted cover letters are an instant disqualification. No matter how good your portfolio, if you can't make the effort to customize the first few lines of your cover letter with something about the company you're applying to, your application immediately goes to the garbage pile.

... BUT DON'T EXPECT ANYONE TO READ PAST THE FIRST LINE

An important follow-up point on the cover letter is that very few people will read past the first sentence, so make sure it's a bloody good line.

MAKE YOUR PORTFOLIO LINK VISIBLE

The link to your portfolio is rally the only thing that matters in your application, so make it as visible as possible. Remember the five-second review rule I mentioned earlier? HR software is clunky, so you'll get bonus points if you include a link to your portfolio in a cover letter, even if you already filled out a special field called "portfolio."

> The link to your portfolio is really the only thing that matters in your application, so make it as visible as possible.

DON'T SEND 30MB PDF FILES

This is another automatic disqualification. If you don't have a website and you decide to clog up inboxes with a giant PDF file, you are not going to win any friends on the creative director's side. Truthfully, if you don't have a good website, you probably aren't ready to be applying for a job anyway. Read about creating your portfolio website on page 34.

INTERVIEW DOS

Knows everything about the company he is meeting

Researched interviewer on LinkedIn and knows them, their work, and the name of their dog

Prepared to ask three or four smart questions

Dresses professionally no matter how creative the company is

Portfolio of his six best projects ready in a presentation on his laptop

INTERVIEW DON'TS

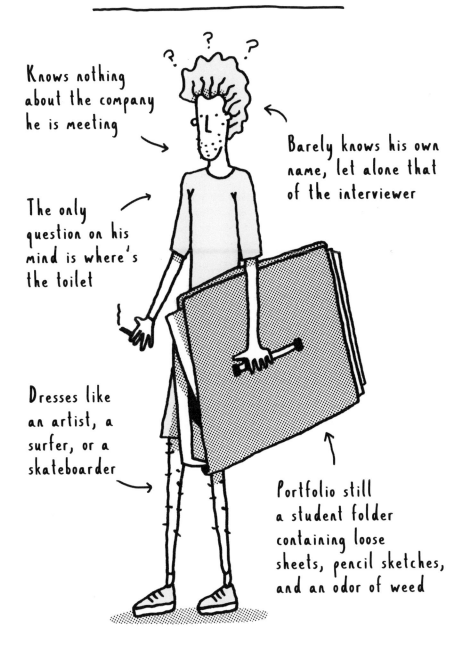

SEND A THANK-YOU NOTE

It's amazing how far good manners go. Follow up every meeting or interview with a "thank you for your time" note, preferably personalized with a reference to something you spoke about in the interview.

FOLLOW UP, BUT DON'T BE ANNOYING

Don't forget to follow up. Unless a different timeline was specified, if you haven't heard anything one week after an interview, it's appropriate to follow up. If you don't hear anything back after that, follow up two weeks later. If nothing after that, forget about them. If a company—no matter how cool they might seem—can't be bothered to reply to job applications, there's a good chance they don't have a great culture and may not be worth working for in the first place.

If you haven't directly applied for a job, and you've just contacted the creative director with a general outreach, follow up in six months and ask to meet up for coffee. Add them to your holiday card list. Send them a note when you add an awesome new project to your portfolio that might actually be interesting for them.

NEGOTIATING YOUR CONTRACT

Assuming you've made it through the above steps and got an offer, then hearty congrats are in order. You have managed to get a first job offer—perhaps even multiple offers if you are really lucky. Here comes the final step of the process: negotiating.

By and large, creative people are worse at negotiating than Mike Tyson is at singing "In the Air Tonight." We are rarely motivated by money alone, and instead are driven by interesting projects and the opportunity to work with great people. It is easy for an unscrupulous company to use these proverbial carrots to take advantage of junior creatives, especially at the salary negotiation stage. It is all too common for the hiring manager to lowball the salary offer with the promise of "great portfolio opportunities," "exciting brands," or, the most patronizing of all, "a chance to work with the best people in the business."

Here's how to put your best foot forward when negotiating:

RESEARCH THE LOCAL SALARY

Conduct thorough research into what to expect in terms of salaries, especially if you're moving to a new city or country. Foreign workers who are on an employer-sponsored work visa are especially vulnerable to being ripped off. For example, a starting salary of $40,000 might seem like a small fortune to a designer coming from certain parts of the world, but it could be that you should be earning well over $70,000. Do your homework.

STATE YOUR EXPECTATIONS UPFRONT

Never be afraid to ask what the salary range for the position is. Better still, communicate your expectations to the company early on, so that you're both on the same page. Keep in mind that the more junior you are, the less negotiating power you have.

IF IN DOUBT, HIGHBALL

If you are lucky enough to be asked what your salary expectations are, be sure to add at least 20-25 percent to whatever the minimum you are willing to accept—no matter how nice the interviewer is. At the risk of sounding like the ever-colorful author of *The Art of the Deal*, negotiating is just part and parcel of landing a job. This is business, after all.

> If you are lucky enough to be asked what your salary expectations are, be sure to add at least 20-25 percent to whatever minimum you are willing to accept

SURVIVE YOUR FIRST JOB

It's the night before your first day at your new job, and you are feeling more than a little anxious. Truth be told, your stomach feels less as if it is filled with butterflies, and more like a stampeding herd of rabid, blind donkeys trampling furiously through your digestive system. Your palms become sweaty, your throat tightens up as you encounter the second crisis of your formative professional years: Imposter Syndrome. Fear not, dear reader; you've already done the hard part by landing that first job, project, or big client.

Here's how not to fuck it up.

PREPARING FOR YOUR FIRST JOB

As the old saying goes: If you fail to prepare, then prepare to fail. If you have followed my sage advice from the previous chapter about the importance of thoroughly researching your potential employer (or client), you will already know a significant amount about who you are going to be working for. If you have not undertaken this exercise, you clearly know better than me, and should return this book to the point of purchase (refunds not guaranteed).

Before you start your new job, complete this checklist to be sure you are sufficiently prepared. Note, the checklist will take under thirty minutes to complete and will prevent you from looking like an idiot on your first day.

ACTUALLY READ THE ONBOARDING DOCUMENTS THEY SENT OVER
Undoubtedly there are a stack of onboarding documents (about how you will be integrated into the company) lying somewhere in your unopened email. You should probably take a few minutes to read them.

RESEARCH WHO IS WHO IN THE COMPANY
There is nothing more embarrassing than being caught out not knowing the name of the company's CEO on your first day. Take five minutes to learn who is running the company, who the creative director is, and who you will be reporting to.

UNDERSTAND HOW THE BUSINESS OPERATES
This task will take no more than ten minutes. It involves a simple search on who the company's clients are and what work they are doing, and checking industry publications for the latest news on the company.

SURVIVING YOUR FIRST DAY

When you arrive on your first day, you must be prepared for one of two scenarios: a) Mindless boredom, because the resourcing team forgot you were arriving and your first project doesn't start for another two weeks; or b) Absolute insanity, because you were hired to fill a gaping hole on a project

that has been understaffed for a while and now needs to be finished in a seemingly impossible turnaround time.

Even if your first "official" project isn't due to start for ages, reach out to your colleagues and offer to help with any menial tasks.

In my ten-plus years of experience of working in and running creative agencies, this is an unmitigable fact regardless of how famous the company is, how many awards it has won, how many staff it has, or how good the resource managers are. Be prepared either to spend a lot of hours pretending to look busy on the company Wiki page, or to lose a few weekends of sleep on an out-of-control project.

It is important to make your mark during those first weeks. Even if your first "official" project isn't due to start for ages, reach out to your colleagues and offer to help with any menial tasks: retouching images for the studio, doing brochure mockups for the design team, capturing behind-the-scenes footage for the art director—it doesn't matter.

MAKE YOURSELF INDISPENSABLE

Assuming that you've made it past your first week without offending anyone, getting fired, squashing the office dog with your car, or deleting the entire server of projects (as an aside, this happened at our agency recently on an unfortunate employee's very first day), then congratulations are in order. It is now time to shift your focus from surviving the job to making yourself indispensable.

Although this may seem like an obvious goal, as a junior creative, your opportunities to do this on projects may not be immediately apparent. After all, you will not be gifted the sexiest project or account in your first week. Chances are you'll be doing a lot of menial tasks on some less-than-premium clients, such as writing banner ad taglines for the world's third most popular anti-worm medicine.

Worry not, dear reader. Here are some ideas for making your skills shine, regardless of how many anti-worm medicine projects you are assigned to:

ROCK EVERY MENIAL TASK AS IF YOUR LIFE DEPENDED ON IT

To a creative director, the tell-tale sign of a junior who is going to rise through the ranks is that they go above and beyond on every task, no matter how menial it may seem. One of the best designers I've ever worked with started out as an intern on my team. I remember giving her a throw-away task: a simple Photoshop mockup of the logo we designed on a box. Not content to take the assignment at face value, she created a full 3D model and an animation of a custom box. The client was so impressed by this that they commissioned a packaging project. This task was the stand-out moment that made her the most sought-after junior designer, and landed her just about every cool project at the agency at the time.

> To a creative director, the tell-tale sign of a junior who is going to rise through the ranks is that they go above and beyond on every task, no matter how menial.

MAKE THE MOST OF "BORING" BRIEFS

Spoiler alert: When you start your career, you are going to get a lot of boring briefs. Banner ads. Lengthy corporate brochures. Assignments that make you want the project, and possibly your own existence, to end immediately. Before you dismiss a boring assignment, remember this: It is much easier to impress on a small, seemingly boring task than on the "perfect" brief or project.

Let me give you an example. When I started working in New York, one of my first tasks was designing a series of digital banner ads for a big financial institution. Now, I hear you—banners and a large corporate client, not exactly the most exciting combination. My first instinct was, quite naturally, that a week of mindless boredom awaited.

However, not being easily deterred, my copywriting partner and I dug deeper into some research on the possibilities. Surprisingly, as it turns out, there are some pretty innovative creative executions using banner ads out there, even in the finance sector—an industry usually considered dry. We took this inspiration and put ourselves to work creating a suite of interactive content and videos that went far beyond the original brief.

How did the client react? They loved it. They were especially excited that we came back with possibilities they didn't even know existed in this format. From what was an original ask for static banner ads, we ended up creating some pretty innovative work.

REALITIES OF YOUR FIRST CREATIVE JOB

Make a lot of work
that never goes anywhere

Get thrown in the
deep end every day

Work on a lot of
unglamorous projects

Have very little
(or zero) guidance

Have to fight to get
on to good projects

Some long hours while
you figure shit out

Remember this: It's easy to do eye-catching work for a sexy sports or drinks brand with great branding and killer assets to work with. Finding opportunities to do great projects with less-than-sexy clients or briefs is a much more admirable skill. It just takes a little effort.

DEMONSTRATE YOUR RELENTLESS ENTHUSIASM WITH "EXTRA CREDIT"

If all else fails, and the project you are working on simply doesn't allow you to showcase your true capabilities, think about including a fresh idea in your presentation as "extra credit."

For the non-advertising readers among you, "extra credit" is a bonus section of a presentation that comes after showing the assigned work. Often encouraged by account directors as a means to sell more work to a client, creative teams usually pour their heart and soul into these extra-credit concepts as a means to show their chops, even if the "real" assignment was less than inspiring. It's a great way to get noticed, especially if a client buys the work.

Keep in mind two key factors to consider for successful extra-credit ideas:

1: Even though it's extra credit, it must still solve a real business problem. It can't just be "cool" or self-serving.

2: Your idea must be accompanied by a cost and plan to make it happen. Otherwise, it's just creative wank and you've wasted your own and the clients' time.

BE PROACTIVE ABOUT THE ASSIGNMENTS YOU WANT

When I was working in New York, there was always a pitch of some kind or another happening in our agency. They were a great way to build up experience, create rapport with the team, and have a chance to work on something outside of the day-to-day work on your usual client or account. The team selection criteria for these pitches was pretty simple: Who was available, and who was interested? Take my advice: Be proactive and ask if you can help out. Not only will it be appreciated by the pitch team (pitches are always understaffed), but it will also help you get face time with creative directors, work on a cool pitch, and gel with the team.

ANNUAL REVIEWS, PROMOTIONS, AND PAY RISES

Assuming that by this stage you haven't fucked up your first day, and have in fact convinced (or fooled) your team into thinking you're indispensable, it's almost time to cash in on your hard work.

WAIT FOR ONE YEAR

The standard interval between salary increases in the creative industries is one year. The only exception is if your role has significantly changed in the time since either your start date or your last annual review (for example, perhaps you have been given more responsibilities). Be patient and gather your thoughts and input for your review meeting.

PROACTIVELY ASK FOR A REVIEW

There is still a surprising number of companies in the creative industries that don't do annual reviews, or that do them on a half-assed basis. This is especially true of smaller companies. If yours doesn't do annual reviews, be sure to request one from your manager, not only to discuss money matters, but also to assess your creative growth within the company.

CLEARLY STATE YOUR GOALS

Being direct is not a skill that creative people often possess, but don't mince your words when it comes to your annual review. Be clear and direct about your professional and personal goals, both inside and outside of the company. For example, if you're not happy with the path you're on as a product designer and want to switch to being a logo designer, be sure to state this—there is nothing worse than waiting until it's too late, then just quitting.

DON'T BE AFRAID TO ASK FOR A RAISE

It is called the creative industry for a reason: Having an open and direct discussion about money is part of the gig. In the famous words of the designer Mike Monteiro, "Fuck you, pay me."

This is easier said than done. For most creatives, asking for a raise presents the most uncomfortable combination of tasks for our ever-insecure personalities: not only talking about money, but talking about yourself and money. What could be worse?

As with negotiating your contract, entering a discussion about a potential raise needs a level head, clear expectations, and the ability to stand your ground. In advance of your meeting, prepare the answers to the following three topics:

Reasons: Arguably the most important part is having solid reasons for requesting a raise. List the accomplishments that you have completed in the past year, especially the times you went above and beyond your job description.

Research: Before you ask for a raise, make sure you know how much is fair for your position, based on the tasks that you actually do every day. Are you a designer doing the tasks of a design director? What is the industry standard for that position based on location, company size, and experience in the role?

Raise: Finally, based on the above information, be clear about how much you want. You can pad a little for negotiation but, unlike your first contract negotiation, generally speaking it's better to ask for an amount that is closer to what you want.

> Entering a discussion about a potential raise needs a level head, clear expectations, and the ability to stand your ground.

No matter how hard you think discussing money is, don't feel alone here. Even the most successful creatives find it difficult. For example, the renowned type designer Erik Spiekermann frequently cites his biggest challenge as "asking for money for his work[4]." If one of the biggest names in the design industry still finds it hard, don't beat yourself up too much about it.

[4] https://www.fastcompany.com/3048599/type-god-erik-spiekermanns-biggest-challenge-asking-for-money

START A
SIDE HUSTLE

Take it from me, dear reader: you will create quite a bit of less-than-inspiring work in the first year or two of your career. This is probably one of the most jarring differences between the comfort of university and the first years of the "real world": You go from self-initiated projects, full creative freedom, and "change-the-world" gusto, to low-level client work—resizing banner ads selling dog food, Photoshopping out the nostril hair of an aging model, or writing taglines for hemorrhoid unguents. In short, the projects you'll be assigned to as a junior creative are quite often spectacularly unglamorous. You may often be left wondering, "Is this it?" Enter the side hustle—your ticket to take your career wherever you want it to go.

THE IMPORTANCE OF THE SIDE HUSTLE

Every creative professional needs a side hustle. It's not just about making more money on the side—it's about you being in the driver's seat of your own career. This is even more relevant during the early years of your career, because a side hustle allows you to take on exactly the type of work you want to do more of, build up the right type of portfolio, and give the creative mind space to play, learn, and evolve.

Not convinced? Think you're too busy? Here's why you need to make time for a side hustle:

YOU LEARN NEW SKILLS THAT CAN IMPROVE YOUR CLIENT WORK

A side hustle allows you to learn new skills that can feed back into client work at a later stage. For example, taking Code School courses at night to build your personal website will quickly mean these new skills can feed into the next client website design project.

There are exceptions to this rule. For example, a designer whose side hustle focusses on the dark art of wombat taxidermy will probably not find many synergies with their day job building apps at an investment bank.

When it comes to getting new work, you will only be asked to do more of the type of work that is already in your portfolio.

YOU STAY CREATIVELY RELEVANT

Side hustles keep your creative skills fresh and ensure that you remain relevant. We have all worked at a place with that one dinosaur who hasn't updated their skillset since 1978. Don't be that person. The only reason they're still employed is because of a covert incident in the 1980s involving the boss, a KISS concert, too much tequila, and a sheep.

YOU BUILD A PORTFOLIO OF THE WORK YOU ACTUALLY WANT TO DO

When it comes to getting new work, you will only be asked to do more of the type of work that is already in your portfolio. That's just the way it works. If your book is filled with taglines for the aforementioned hemorrhoid unguents, it's likely that you'll get more work in the area of anal medication (if you're lucky, you might snag a varicose veins campaign). Break the cycle by starting a side hustle that focuses on the work you actually want to do, and fill your portfolio with that.

YOU STAY ETERNALLY YOUNG (AT LEAST CREATIVELY)

Creative play and learning keep us fresh. Remember when you figured out photo editing during an all-nighter with a pirate copy of Photoshop that you "borrowed" from a friend? The learning leaps were huge back then, in no small part due to a lack of worries about timelines and clients. If you want to maintain these leaps of learning (and stay creatively young), you must fumble about, make mistakes, and play with new things without fear of failure. This is sometimes known as "serious play."

"SERIOUS PLAY" AND HOW IT WORKS

The renowned graphic designer Paula Scher coined the phrase "serious play" during her 2008 TED[5] talk to describe creative experimentation. Explaining it, she drew the distinction between serious play and solemn play. Serious play can be explained as the naive first time of learning something new and not being afraid to make mistakes in the process. Solemn play, however, often occurs when one has to fulfill a requirement in a fixed way, or when one is asked to recreate a style or technique that was once "serious play," but in a solemn manner. Interestingly, solemn play can still lead to a good result, but the naivety of learning and playful exploration is gone.

Scher gave some examples to illustrate the difference between serious and solemn play: "Children are serious, adults are solemn. Poker is serious. Jogging is solemn. New York is serious. Washington, D.C., is solemn." You get the picture. In the summary of her TED talk, Scher discussed the "staircase of creative learning"—going from short and high steps in the teens and twenties, with the steps gradually becoming wider and smaller as one gets older. Learning naturally occurs fastest when you're younger and have the most to learn; as individuals grow older they become more solemn and their willingness for new learning slows down.

To remain creatively fresh, playing with new toys, tools, and methods must become part of your process. I've worked with designers with personal projects from watercolor paintings to travel hacking, building their own furniture to running cooking blogs. It doesn't matter what it is, in order to stay fresh and create relevant work, you must make space to grow via your own personal projects.

5 https://www.ted.com/talks/paula_scher_great_design_is_serious_not_solemn

CAREER—BUILDING SIDE HUSTLES

GOOD HUSTLE

Doesn't feel
like a day job

Learn something
completely new

Pushes your portfolio in
the right direction

BAD HUSTLE

Fills you with
feelings of dread

Repeat shit you've
done before

Zero relevance to your
career goals

HOW TO GET STARTED, FROM ZERO TO SIDE HUSTLE

I can hear the whining already.

"But I'm already slammed in my real job!"
"Where will I get time for this?"
"I have to walk my tortoise."
"I need time to binge-watch *Keeping Up with the Kardashians.*"

Calm yourself. Read on.

KEEP IT SLOW AND STEADY

It sounds counter-productive, but don't be over-ambitious. The real secret to getting shit done is taking a slow and steady approach. For example, let's look at this book (the very definition of a side hustle). This time, I set myself a goal to write for a minimum of fifteen minutes per day, if nothing else. Now, this may not sound like much, but let's look at the math. Fifteen minutes translates to about 300 words. If I am consistent with this (and if you are reading this, we can assume that I have been), I would have around 25,000 words—i.e. a first draft of this book—entirely completed in about three months, at a very relaxed pace indeed.

Repeat: Slow and steady.

IT CAN'T FEEL LIKE WORK

First things first—your side hustle must be separate from your day-to-day work. It can, of course, use the same skills as you do in work (e.g. if you are a photographer by day, there's nothing wrong with your side hustle being photography-related), but it shouldn't feel like work.

Allow me to give you an example. For a period, when I was working in New York, my day-to-day job as an art director mostly centered on one large financial account. While the account itself was not a bad one, I nonetheless needed a means of self-expression outside of promoting the merits of one wealth-management strategy versus another. So, in October 2016, my colleague Kevin Growick and I decided to set up *Adloids*, a satirical online publication focussed on ripping apart the ad industry in which we worked (think *The Onion* of advertising). It was fun to make, almost therapeutic, and, above all else, it felt nothing like work.

PAIR UP WITH SOMEONE

When it comes to starting a self-initiated project, motivation is often the biggest problem. The easiest way to get around your inner sloth is to partner with someone on your side hustle. Having another person keeps you motivated when you feel like giving up, and brings a fresh set of eyes into the equation. With *Adloids*, we would not have launched anything if there hadn't been two of us doing it.

SET A DEADLINE

Add a layer of accountability to your project. Draw a line in the sand and make a launch date. Much as you did with your portfolio, communicate it publicly so that you are accountable to someone other than yourself. For Adloids, we announced it on our social media channels weeks before it was even live.

JUST LAUNCH THE DAMN THING

Just like launching your portfolio, the worst enemy preventing you from turning your side hustle from vague notion into reality is the desire for perfection. When we launched *Adloids*, we had only five articles and about a zillion bugs. No one noticed.

SIDE-HUSTLE ANALYSIS

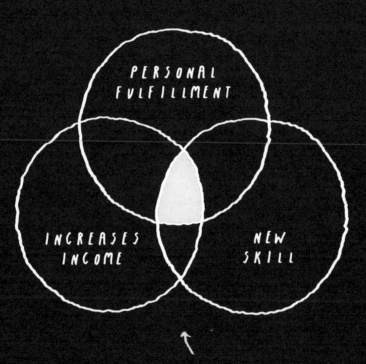

At least <u>one</u> is required

GET PAID TO TRAVEL

I will let you in on a little secret: If you work in the creative industries, not only can you travel the world as part of your career, but people will pay you to do so. It is quite possibly the greatest (and often most underused) perk of our industry. Whether you are a designer, a writer, a filmmaker, or even a dog hairstylist, creative skills are more in demand than ever, and with the rise of remote work, it is easier than ever to get paid to travel the world.

TRAVEL IN THE CREATIVE INDUSTRIES

I have been extremely fortunate when it comes to paid travel. It started shortly after I had graduated from university, when I was offered an internship at a prestigious design firm with a difficult-to-pronounce name, based in Berlin. What I didn't know at the time was that this three-month stint would be the start of over a decade of professional travel in the creative industries, spanning Berlin, London, South Africa, New York, and, at the time of writing, Los Angeles. I never looked back.

Sometimes I need to pinch myself about how lucky I've been. I've never had to pay a penny to move either myself or my belongings (including my ever-stubborn basset hound) between countries or cities, worry about getting a visa, pay an apartment deposit, or even pay the cost of a flight. Getting paid to travel the world is one of the greatest perks of working in the creative industries. Only an idiot would not take advantage of it, at least once.

Beyond its merits as a recreational pursuit, working abroad is essential if you want to be a world-class creative professional. Travel opens the mind to different ways of working and fundamentally changes the way you think about the world. It gives you multiple perspectives from which to think about a problem or challenge. Whenever I'm hiring a designer and I see from their resumé that they've only worked in their hometown for the past ten years, it gives me pause: They have only one perspective on the world, and no matter how good that perspective is, it is a very narrow one.

Travel opens the mind to different ways of working and fundamentally changes the way you think about the world.

So, you've decided that a career abroad is for you. But where do you start?

STARTING A TRAVEL PLAN

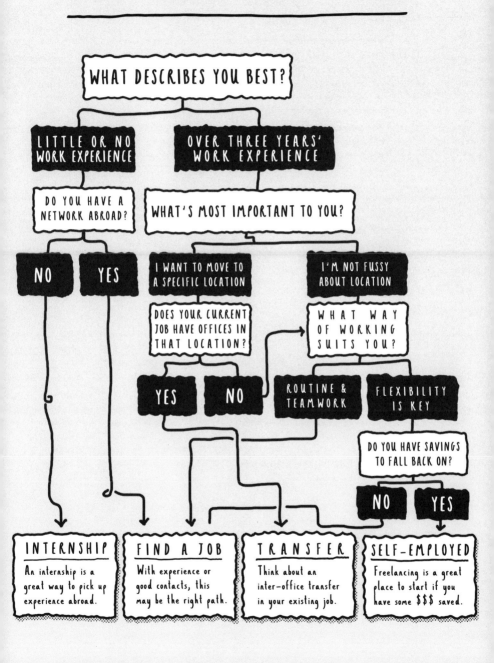

PLOTTING YOUR COURSE

Unless you are already flooded with head-hunters calling at the door with offers, or have a vast family inheritance leaving you free to swan around the cities of the world pretending to be an artist, you must factor the real practicalities of budget, level of experience, and network of connections into your travel plans.

For the purposes of this book, I am assuming that you, dear reader, are not the heir to the throne of Saudi Arabia, and that your plans to travel must be based on reality, return on investment, and practicality. For example, I would have loved to have moved to New York or LA for my first internship, but the reality was that I simply could not afford to.

With this in mind, your move abroad should start with these steps:

STEP 1:
DECIDE IF THE LOCATION OR THE JOB IS MORE IMPORTANT

The first thing you need to be clear about when plotting your career abroad is identifying what is most important to you. Generally speaking, there are two mindsets when it comes to starting a career abroad:

THE LOCATION IS THE DRIVING FORCE IN YOUR DECISION
In this case, you want to work in a certain place, but the specific job there is flexible. For example, when I left Berlin for New York in 2014, my wife and I knew we wanted to live in New York. Therefore, I tailored my job hunting around this city and nowhere else, regardless of what opportunities arose in other locations.

THE ROLE IS THE DRIVING FORCE IN YOUR DECISION
In other cases, the most important thing is the type of work. For example, when I applied for my internship at Edenspiekermann in Berlin, I knew I wanted to work in a prestigious agency in another country, but the location didn't matter. The role was the driving factor.

Of course, there are those rare people who are clear about what they want to do as well as where they want to do it. My brother wanted to be a fashion photographer in New York and was single-minded in his determination to get there. Side note: I am jealous of these types of people, because my path has mostly involved bumbling from one thing to the next.

STEP 2:
PLAN WHAT YOU WANT TO DO

The next big decision is what you want to do in your soon-to-be new homeland. Your options will depend a lot on your personal experience, the existence of a network of connections (or lack thereof) in your desired location, and, of course, your budget. Again, for the purposes of this book, we are assuming that you have limited (if any) personal connections that could land you a job right away, and a limited budget. If you did, after all, you probably wouldn't have made me 20 bucks richer by buying this book.

With all that in mind, your options will probably look something like this:

YOU COULD GET A JOB WORKING AT A COMPANY
This is probably the most common route. The benefits are that someone else is handling the hard part—the visa, a stable source of income, most likely some relocation costs, and perhaps even temporary accommodation while you get set up. Keep in mind, however, that from an employer's perspective, hiring overseas employees is tremendously time-consuming and expensive because of the need to acquire a visa. In this scenario, you will need to demonstrate above-average skills for a company to fork out for airfare, visa, and a whole fucking mountain of paperwork.

YOU COULD DO AN INTER-COMPANY TRANSFER TO YOUR DESIRED LOCATION
This is an option that is not always obvious, but actually is one of the easiest routes to living abroad. Instead of looking for a new job abroad, look for a role in your home country at a company that has a global footprint. I have a lot of friends who have done this for big tech companies, and it is, hands down, the easiest way. I had a friend in Europe who really wanted to live in Brooklyn, but didn't have a direct route there. Instead, he got a job at a big tech company in Europe and transferred to Brooklyn after almost three years in the London office.

THE DOS AND DON'TS OF YOUR VISA INTERVIEW

DO ...

Gather all your shit into a single folder

Practice with test questions

Dress professionally

DON'T ...

Bring literally anything into the embassy

Make jokes

Wear a disguise

The only downside is that this is a long game, in that you must first prove yourself and build up loyalty in the company. Additionally, inter-company transfer visas usually require you to have worked at the same company in your home country for some time. For example, the inter-company transfer visa for the US—known as the L1— requires employees to have worked at the company for at least one year before they are eligible to apply.

YOU COULD START YOUR OWN COMPANY

If you have some clients and financial backup, you could take the leap and open your own company. Certainly this comes with many perks—you are your own boss, you can do things on your own schedule, and in general act like someone who is very important. However, this is a difficult endeavor for a first step in a career abroad. You will need financial backing. Tax laws vary widely between countries. Perhaps most challenging, you are on your own when it comes to getting a visa. Unless you already run a successful business in your home country and want to make the leap to another location, it is this author's opinion that this path is best avoided for the first-time expat, and is almost definitely not suitable for the recent graduate.

YOU COULD FREELANCE

While this is undoubtedly another tough route from a visa perspective, becoming a freelancer means that you really can make your own luck— especially in the current age of remote work. A tip for those not sure where to begin: Start by working remotely with existing clients from your home country, then slowly build a new roster of clients in parallel.

YOU COULD LOOK FOR AN INTERNSHIP

All the above options require a certain level of experience. The trade-off is, of course, money. While it is this author's opinion that all internships should be paid, the reality of the creative industries means that this is not always the case. However, getting an internship in an unfamiliar country is considerably easier than finding a full-time job.

YOU COULD START BY STUDYING ABROAD TO BUILD YOUR NETWORK

A viable alternative for those of you without a network or work experience is to take a year and study abroad. While this option certainly does not fulfill the promise of this chapter of travelling for free, it is a viable option to consider if all the above options fail.

Regardless of which path you pick, the next part of your process is the real baptism of fire: obtaining a visa.

STEP 3: GET A VISA

Using the map of hell from Dante's *Inferno*, navigate past the panderers, the hypocrites, and the thieves, and traverse to the very deepest level of the underworld. There you will find a special place reserved for officials from the immigration bureaus in charge of handling work visas for immigrants. Ask anyone about the work visa process and their face will turn gray, and they will visibly age approximately ten years before your eyes. There are not enough pages here to describe the inanity of the process, and perhaps the less said the better. But allow me to briefly illustrate some of the challenges for you.

Getting a work visa is more painful than a root canal without anesthetic. Let's say, for example, that you want to get a visa for the USA and you are one of the lucky ones—you have found an employer to sponsor your visa. Not only that, but you have six degrees, including a doctorate from the finest college in your homeland. Maybe you've won a Nobel Prize. Perhaps you've even created a cure for cancer. Surely you'll have an easy path to a visa? Think again. The visa gatekeepers of U.S. Citizenship and Immigration Services have no mercy and give zero shits about you.

As someone who has done it not once, but three times, I can say this: Getting a work visa is more painful than a root canal without anesthetic (and believe me, I know what that is like—I had one when I lived in Berlin at a Soviet-era dentist in the East of the city). All that being said, there are a few things that can make the process a bit easier.

THE SECRET TO GETTING A VISA
The real trick is that getting a visa starts before you ever think you'll need one. When you're at school, you might think that you'll never need a visa. This is a myth. If you are a creative professional who is looking to be at the top of your game, chances are that you will need one at some stage.

STAY IN SCHOOL—ACTUALLY FINISH YOUR DEGREE
This counts for a lot. Despite increasingly popular opinions in the creative industries to shun traditional college learning in favor of YouTube tutorials, there is no denying that having a "real" degree automatically qualifies you for multiple categories of visa (for example, the H1B in the USA). If you're lucky enough to be able to afford further education, stick it out and finish your degree.

THE TRAVEL CHECKLIST

☐ Do a test trip to the new city

☐ Allow at least six months to get a visa

☐ Check local salary expectations to be sure that you're getting a fair deal

☐ Negotiate for a relocation allowance

☐ Save enough cash reserves for three months

☐ Cull your personal crap to the bare minimum

☐ Research tax laws beforehand

☐ Set up a healthcare plan

☐ Learn at least the basics of the language

☐ Join a local creative network in advance

Failure to fully complete this list will result in anxiety, stress, hair loss, weight gain, hemorrhoids, and failed travel plans.

START WRITING, TODAY

There is no easier way to show a visa authority that you are qualified for a talent-based visa than to establish yourself as an authority in industry publications. The real secret is that creative publications are always looking for industry contributors for columns, tutorials, and general opinions. I started my writing career producing posts for our company blog, and in all honesty I would not have obtained a single visa had I not started on this path.

INDUSTRY AWARDS HELP (UNFORTUNATELY)

There is no one on the planet who hates the self-congratulatory, patting-each-other-on-the-back, pay-to-play BS that are creative awards more than me. Unfortunately, no matter how silly they are, awards always look good on a visa application. Whenever there is an opportunity for a well-respected award (even if it is pay-to-play), consider entering it, especially if it's early in your career.

GETTING PAID TO TRAVEL

Speaking as someone who runs a creative agency, getting someone a visa is a headache even for big companies. Before you expect an employer to arrange a visa, bear in mind that they will only do it if the person is a) truly exceptional, and b) going to stay with the agency for at least three years. Remember this when you ask a company to fill in three hundred pages of visa paperwork for you.

A final note on getting paid to travel. Be patient. Apply for many jobs and allow yourself enough time. Above all, be prepared, and remember that the first step in a career abroad is by far the hardest. Be ready to take an opportunity, even if the job is not perfect; you can always change roles in a few years. As someone who has spent over a decade getting paid to live all around the world, let me promise you one thing: It is worth the effort.

NOT ALL THOSE WHO WANDER ARE LOST

J.R.R. TOLKIEN

UNLESS, OF COURSE, YOU ARE ACTUALLY LOST

MASTER THE BORING SH*T

I can hear the complaining already. Money? Contracts? Taxes? This is supposed to be a book on the creative industries, Paul—what is this crap? At the risk of sounding like Grampa Simpson, if I could give one piece of advice to my twenty-something-year-old self it would be this: Learn how the business shit works before it bites you in the ass (and it will). Business basics can be the difference between a great creative professional who makes a lot of money and an equally great creative professional who doesn't. There are literally hundreds of detailed books on the subject of business for creatives. Before you dive head-first into your career, you should read at least one of them. Read this chapter if nothing else. I promise I'll keep it short.

THE IMPORTANCE OF BUSINESS FOR CREATIVES

When it comes to "the boring shit," creative people—especially when we're early in our careers—are notorious for putting all on the back burner and focussing exclusively on The Work. After all, we deliberately side-stepped the mind-numbingly dull subjects like business, finance, and economics when we selected art school in our college applications. To make matters worse, many design and creative schools don't even teach business basics[6], a fact that is mind-boggling. Overall, this leads to a significant gap in professional knowledge, one that isn't nearly so common in any other consulting profession.

Whether you like it or not, having basic business know-how is crucial to a successful creative career. All too often, this is a fact that many don't realize until something goes wrong: when a shady client vanishes without paying as soon as you've naively handed over the deliverables without taking a prepayment, for example. Or maybe it'll be when a project goes wildly out of control because there is no contract specifying a list of deliverables. Or, worst of all, perhaps you get embroiled in a legal dispute because you didn't license something correctly. Nobody wants these situations to happen, but they do and they will. The vast majority can be prevented with better management up front.

Having basic business know-how is crucial to a successful creative career

THE BASICS

There are four topics that, in this author's humble opinion, every creative needs to be familiar with. You don't need to do all of these yourself, but you need to be aware of how they work, and who can handle them for you.

They are:
- Pricing
- Scoping
- Writing contracts
- Accounting and legal shit

[6] https://www.davidairey.com/graphic-design-schools

PRICING

How much do I charge? How much will they pay me? Let's be honest, this is the one thing that every freelance creative wants to know. The good news is that figuring this out is far from rocket science.

Here is a simple formula to calculate what you should be charging a client for your work:

1. Add up your work expenses
First things first. How much does it cost to do your job? Factor in everything from your home office rent to the little yellow pencils sitting in the jar on your desk.

Example:

Home office	$5,000
Phone/internet	$2,000
Printing	$500
Office supplies	$500
Travel	$5,000
Total yearly overhead costs:	**$13,000**

2. Figure out how much you want to make per year
This is the fun part: How much do you want to earn as a salary per year? Don't forget to research the market rate so that what you charge is grounded in reality and is competitive. Websites like Glassdoor and Working Not Working frequently post salary and freelance guides for most creative roles.

Example:
After your research, you decide that $80,000 per year is reasonable and competitive for what you're offering.

3. Add the two to get your total costs
Add the two totals above to get your total costs.

Example:

Overhead costs	$13,000
Salary	$80,000
Total costs	**$93,000**

COMMON PRICING QUESTIONS

Can you give me a discounted hourly rate because I'm a new client?	→ My rate is based on costs. Instead I can offer a first project discount of 2%.
That seems like a lot. Couldn't I get this work cheaper on a crowdsourced site?	→ Good work is an investment. Here's how it will impact your bottom line ...
Could you do this for exposure instead of money?	→ Let's talk. Based on real numbers, how much do you estimate this to be worth?
There's more work down the line if you do this one for free	→ Fuck off

4. Figure out how many hours per year you can bill

The amount you charge your client should also factor in the days when you're not billing them. For example, this includes administration days when you are handling invoicing or marketing yourself, doing pitches, etc. Additionally, you will need to factor in vacation days, sick days, and any other time when you are not directly "billable" to a client.

Example:

Potential working days per year	260
Public holidays	-10
Vacation days	-20
Sick days	-5
Non-billable working days (admin, internal, PR, etc.)	-52
Actual billable days per year:	173

5. Calculate your hourly rate

Now comes the math. To get the daily rate that you charge your clients, simply divide your costs by the number of days you can bill.

Example:
$93,000 (total costs) ÷ 173 (billable days) = $537.57
Your daily rate is (rounded up for convenience): $550

A NOTE ON NON-MONETARY COMPENSATION

One of the most frequently asked questions by young creatives is "Should I ever work for non-monetary compensation, or even for free?" Let's be clear, these are two very different things. You should never work for free. Period. Your time has value, and people are willing to pay for this. With that out of the way, what about when a non-monetary payment is offered?

Non-monetary compensation can be any type of payment that is not hard dollars. A client may try and entice you to work for exposure, equity in their company, a lifetime supply of the hemorrhoid unguents that you are designing the packaging for—the list goes on. There is nothing wrong with working for non-monetary compensation, on a project that simply doesn't yet have the hard cash (e.g. a startup or a charity). However, it is crucial to review this type of offer carefully to separate the bullshit from the real opportunities and quantify the effort in advance.

WHAT'S THE BEST WAY TO SCOPE?

FIXED PRICE

Perfect when you can predict the outcome

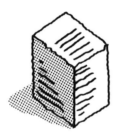

Detailed contracting is required

Easy to go over-budget & hard to change scope

TIME-BASED

Better for complex projects with unknowns

TIMESHEETS

11.4 seconds

Detailed time-tracking is needed

No.

Difficult to sell this approach to clients

To do this, firstly you need to scope the work and estimate how many hours you will be doing, as with any regular project. This allows you to put a very clear dollar amount against it. Communicate this clearly.

The second part is to establish if the non-monetary compensation that was offered matches that value. Sometimes this is easy, such as getting product samples, or getting shares in a startup based on the dollar amount (be sure to factor in an extra percentage for the risk you are taking). At other times, it's trickier—such as when a client comes to you and offers "exposure." For full transparency, this author does not believe in working for exposure because more often than not there is very little quantifiable outcome. That being said, if you have a product to sell, and can put a definite monetary value on the exposure (for example, a feature on a particular blog will lead to 100 book sales), it may be worth considering. In this case, be sure to get all the hard data on how many people the "exposure" will reach, and what the monetary result will be based on similar past partnerships. But the big brand that asks for free work in exchange for "exposure"? Forget it.

SCOPING

Now that you know how much to charge, it's time to scope your first project. There are two basic ways to do this:

1. By time: You sell hours rather than deliverables.
2. By price: You give a fixed price for a defined list of tasks.

There is no right or wrong method. As a guideline, if you are working with something that has a lot of unknowns—for example, designing a large website for which you don't yet know the page count—billing by the hour is the safest option, so that you are not locked into delivering for a fixed price. But (and it's a big but) most clients do not like time-based projects. The lack of a fixed list of deliverables describing what they can expect for their money makes them extremely nervous.

If you're confident that you know enough about the project to accurately price a list of deliverables—for example, a recurring job that you do every year for a client—a fixed price is probably the right choice. The caveat here is that every fixed-price project must be meticulously scoped, otherwise you will quickly run into trouble.

Here are the main points to keep in mind when scoping a fixed-price project:

SPECIFY EVERY DETAIL TO THE LETTER
Fixed-price projects run into problems when either side is unclear about what is and what is not included in the project. There is no such thing as being too detailed in your contract. More on this in a moment.

ADD A CONTINGENCY FOR THINGS GOING WRONG
Remember that the laws of the universe dictate that whatever can go wrong, will go wrong. Factor in a contingency to your pricing for unexpected developments by adding a 10 percent buffer time.

IF IN DOUBT, INSIST ON A TIME-BASED SCOPE INSTEAD
If there is any doubt about exactly what you will deliver in the project, do not take the risk, no matter how attractive or tantalizing the brand may be. Unless you and the client can agree on the exact deliverables that can be specified in the contract, do not proceed. If you can't agree, a time-based project is the best option.

WRITING CONTRACTS

The contract with your client—referred to as a "Statement of Work" (SOW for short)—is where you list every detail of the engagement. It is impossible to overstate the importance of getting this document right. Rushing this step will run the risk of a whole host of problems: not getting paid, never-ending client feedback resulting in a grossly over-budget project, breakdown of a client relationship, mental anguish, despair, and quite possibly the eventual onset of piles. It's really important.

Here are the things you need to include in your client contracts:

LIST OF DELIVERABLES
First and foremost, you must include the full details of the project, and whether it's a fixed-price scope or a time-based scope. If you're working with a fixed-price scope with fixed deliverables, there is no such thing as being too granular when scoping a project. Your contract should state exactly what is and is not included, how many rounds of feedback there will be, when things will be delivered, and in what format.

INGREDIENTS OF A CONTRACT

Statement of work

Deliverables

- —————
- —————
- —————

- —————
- —————
- —————

- —————
- —————
- —————

Detailed breakdown of deliverables

Costs

—————
—————

Itemized costs

Payment terms

- —————
- —————

- —————
- —————

When you get paid and how

Terms & conditions

- —————
- —————

- —————
- —————

Disclaimers

Glossary

- —————
- —————

- —————
- —————

Definition of terminology

Signatures

——————   ——————

The most important part

When providing deliverables, be specific to a fault. For example:

1. We will create two design directions of the new website that will be presented in a Keynote deck via video call.
2. Each design direction will include the homepage and the contact page, as well as a moodboard of the concept.
3. Following the presentation, the client will choose one direction.
4. The client will provide two rounds of feedback on the chosen website concept. Additional feedback rounds can be provided on a time and materials basis.
5. Approval of final concept will be provided in writing.
6. Final deliverable will consist of Sketch file with website designs for the homepage and contact page. These will be designed at desktop, tablet, and cell sizes and will be delivered within two weeks of concept sign-off.

SPECIFY WHAT IS NOT INCLUDED

Be sure to include a clause that states that third-party costs—for example, travel, stock photography, illustrations, etc.—are not included in your price.

TIMELINE

Make your life easier by including a detailed timeline in every contract that includes presentations, deliverables, and when the client's feedback is due.

DETAILED BREAKDOWN OF COSTS

Provide a full breakdown of all costs involved in the project. Set this out in as much detail as possible so that your potential client can see exactly how the costs were calculated. Transparency always wins—no one likes surprise costs down the line.

PREPAYMENT SCHEDULE

Repeat after me: "I will never work on a freelance project without a prepayment." A prepayment is your safety net if something goes wrong. Unfortunately, many clients are of the mind that the creative should shoulder the burden of responsibility and work in "good faith," only receiving a payment when final assets are handed over. Pro tip: If a client isn't willing to provide a prepayment, it's an immediate red flag.

How you should break down a prepayment depends on your relationship with the client and the length of the project:

New client:
50% up front, 50% billed on completion

Existing client short project (up to two months):
30% up front, 70% billed on completion

Existing client long project (more than two months):
30% up front, the remainder divided by month and billed monthly

PAYMENT TERMS
Be sure to include the details of your payment terms (i.e. when your invoices are due). While it's nice to get a "Due upon receipt" agreement for invoices, in reality, Net 30 days is the standard payment terms across most industries; larger corporations may be as much as Net 60, and for government clients a Net 90 payment term is not uncommon.

ACCOUNTING AND LEGAL DETAILS

This is the one part of the business where my advice is to leave it to the professionals. Before you start working freelance it is imperative that you do the following: Get a good accountant and get a good lawyer. Believe it or not, both are a lot cheaper than you probably think, and they are a lot cheaper than the repercussions of not having them when something goes wrong. When selecting a lawyer or accountant, be sure to choose someone who works with creatives in your industry. You'll thank me in a few years.

Before you start working freelance it is imperative that you do the following: Get a good accountant and get a good lawyer.

ONE MORE THING

That's it for the boring stuff. Not so bad, right? You'll be a business guru in no time. Now, not to alarm you, but there's just one last aspect of the business side of the creative industries left to cover. This is the one that strikes terror into the heart of creatives: The Client. Read on.

LEARN TO MANAGE CLIENTS

The client. A creature of lore that strikes fear into the heart of even the bravest newbie creative. The Grim Reaper of good ideas, the Destroyer of great work. Our industry is filled with tales of the ongoing friction between frustrated creatives and their seemingly clueless clients. Now, before you dismiss the behavior of a client as just being "difficult," remember this: While managing difficult clients can be a true skill, it is the creative process itself that is to blame. Mastering the art of client management will make your life easier, your work better, and your bank balance considerably higher.

THE PROBLEM BETWEEN CREATIVES AND CLIENTS

All too often, junior creatives approach the task of producing work in isolation, much like an artist painting the ceiling of the Sistine Chapel or a ninth-century monk transcribing the Bible in a dark cave for years on end. They give zero thought to how much it costs or how long it takes, as long as it is a great piece of work. The mindset is a simple binary one: Great work good, good work bad. Realities such as budget, timeline, and actual production don't matter. And there is nothing that pisses off a client more than this.

I still vividly remember the first (and last) time I thought the apparent "greatness" of my work would supersede the realities of delivering a client project on time and on budget. The incident—which I now refer to as "The Highland Affair"—involved a branding project, a close call with a production deadline, and an almost murderous Scottish project manager called Duncan MacDongledropper.

At the time, I was a junior designer, fresh out of school and fully convinced that I was going to change the world with every pixel I pushed. The project in question was a relatively simple one: Create three logo concepts for a new health-food startup, a task I had thrown myself into for weeks on end, burning hours upon hours of budget on noodling, restarts, and general procrastination. By the morning of the client presentation, I had already missed two internal reviews and avoided repeated emails requesting an update, and, needless to say, Duncan—a hot-headed fellow at the best of times—was now extremely irritated.

About thirty minutes before the deadline for sending out the work, Duncan arrived at my desk looking for the presentation. I should have noticed that he was already bordering on a murderous rage—visibly purple-faced and with small flecks of saliva beginning to appear on either side of his jowly mouth. However, lost in my blissful "change the world with design" mentality, I blithely told him I needed at least another two hours to get the work where it needed to be, fully convinced that once the client saw how great it was, all would be forgiven. Big mistake.

To say that Duncan exploded is an understatement. Slamming his fist on my desk so violently that all my pens were ejected from their jar like little

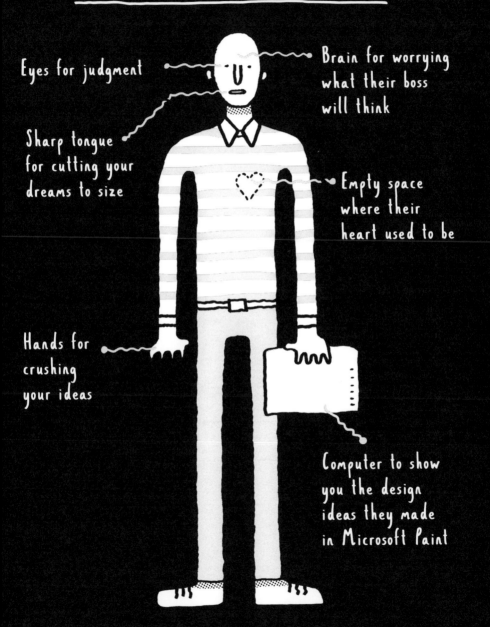

rocket ships going into orbit, I was immediately and permanently shaken from the blissful state of youth with the roar of a thick Scottish accent in my ear.

"Ye wee jobbie!*" he roared. "Ye hud three bludy weeks tae do this presentation an' you bin sittin' on yer arse dickin' arooond for fuck knows how long."

Duncan now leaned in closer to the point and lowered his voice.

"Now see here, sonny—you'll send me that presentation in ten minutes or you'll be out the door with a kick up yer arse."

And sure enough, I did. The presentation was finished in a record time of eight minutes and it was out to the client before the deadline. Surprisingly, I was not fired (although I certainly should have been), and I went on to work with Duncan several times again. The lesson learned: Don't miss a deadline and never mess with a Scottish project manager.

*For those who don't know, "jobbie" is Scottish slang for feces or excrement.

THINGS CLIENTS CARE ABOUT

Your client is not there to fuck up your creative work, your weekend plans, or your career. The reality is that they have a boss, internal politics, and a whole pile of shit on their own plate that you are unaware of. Perhaps they have put their neck on the line to do this project, and have now placed their whole-hearted trust in you. So, when dealing with clients, keep in mind that there are several things they care about more than the perfect logo, tagline, or any other creative output:

CLIENTS CARE ABOUT NOT GETTING FIRED
First and foremost, your client does not want to lose their job—a very real possibility if you mess up, especially for those who work at large corporations where mistakes are not tolerated. If they do not deliver, do not deliver on time, or deliver over budget, they may get fired.

CLIENTS CARE ABOUT KEEPING WITHIN BUDGET
Budget is a real thing. Don't assume that because you burned the entire amount in the first week doing 119 versions of the concept, you'll get more.

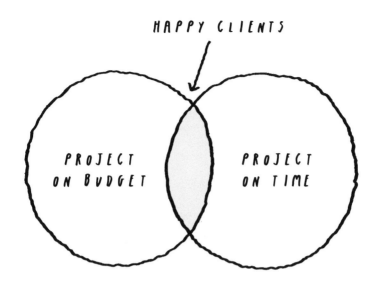

Your project may be one of many the client needs to get done within a finite sum, and once they go over that—well, see point number one.

CLIENTS CARE ABOUT GETTING WORK ON TIME

In my experience, this is the fastest way to get fired by a client (short of ruining the entire project or driving over their beloved chihuahua). No matter how relaxed or friendly a client seems, they will immediately transform into a raging beast when you miss a deadline.

CLIENTS CARE ABOUT IMPRESSING THEIR BOSS

Your client is a person with a boss. They want to look good in front of them. They want a good performance review at the end of the year. They want a bonus so they can take their kids on vacation. Your job is to help them achieve these goals, not just to think about whether their logo should be dark blue or very dark blue.

CLIENTS CARE ABOUT GREAT WORK TOO

Don't get me wrong, most clients care about great work as much as you do. But keep in mind that what constitutes great work from their side is how well it achieves the business goals, not how pretty it looks.

> No matter how relaxed or friendly a client seems, they will immediately transform into a raging beast when you miss a deadline.

CLIENT BASICS

Working with clients is not a dark art, but there are some basics that must be adhered to. Above all else, you need to build their trust. The more trust they have in you, the more productive the relationship will be. When they trust you, they will not micromanage you. They will take more risks when it comes to creative ideas. They will pay you more money because they know you will not fail them. Above all else, they will let you do the job they hired you for.

Here are some ways to build that trust, and create a partnership that produces great work and a happy client:

Stick to the mantra of an old colleague of mine: No brief, no work.

WRITE A BRIEF BEFORE YOU DO ANYTHING

Stick to the mantra of an old colleague of mine: No brief, no work. Do not waver from these words under any circumstances. Furthermore, even if the client does provide briefing, it is always a good idea to write a rebrief to ensure that it makes sense to you and the other creatives working on it. Most importantly, get this rebrief signed off by the client before you start work.

BE CLEAR ABOUT WHO THE DECISION-MAKER IS

Nothing gets done if it is designed by committee. Far too many client–creative relationships break down when there is a lack of clarity about who is accountable and who calls the shots.

Too many client–creative relationships break down when there is a lack of clarity about who is accountable and who calls the shots.

My favorite example of this is a website project we did a few years ago for a client with three founders, each one more ego-driven than the next. The real challenge lay in the fact that not one of them was willing to cede control of the project. After every single creative presentation, each of the three founders would phone me separately, one after another, all with different opinions and feedback requests on the work we had delivered. After weeks of burning the budget and chasing our tails without making any progress, we finally told them they needed to get their act together or we would fire them. It worked: After this intervention, the trio delivered consolidated feedback in one Google Doc, and working with them went relatively smoothly for the rest of the project.

Remember: There can be only one decision-maker, and that must be clearly established before you start work.

ENFORCE A STRUCTURED FEEDBACK PROCESS

When it comes to the work itself, nothing irks a client more than feeling that their feedback was not listened to. However, all too often, clients deliver feedback in an inconsistent and non-actionable manner. Make it easier by sending them these ground rules at the outset of the project.

All feedback on creative work must be:

–Delivered in writing
While discussing creative work in a presentation is all well and good, all feedback must be delivered in writing. This holds both the creative and the client accountable. If something isn't clear, it is the creative's responsibility to request clarification. If something isn't there, it doesn't get done.

–Consolidated
A frequent challenge with written feedback happens when various parties from the client provide individual, sometimes conflicting, feedback. Eliminate this problem by insisting that all client feedback is consolidated into one document, with one clear direction.

–Constructive:
Instead of ambiguous statements such as "Make this advertisement for hemorrhoid cream more EPIC," be clear: "The plain white background makes this ad too boring and doesn't attract attention. Let's try a version that includes a photo of a real hemorrhoid."

Underpromise and overdeliver, never the other way around.

–Include examples
Nothing makes feedback more actionable than including an example. If a piece of client feedback is still unclear, ask them to provide an example of what they meant.

NEVER MISS A DEADLINE

This is a lesson hard learnt from past experiences of biting off more than I could chew: Underpromise and overdeliver, never the other way around. There is nothing that will annoy a client more than not delivering when you say you will, whether you are late by a minute, a day, or a month. Repeat after me: I will not miss a deadline.

DON'T COMPETE WITH THEIR IN-HOUSE TEAMS

In recent years, there has been a huge trend of insourcing creative onto the client side. Be it design, marketing, or video production, the people on the other side of the table are increasingly as talented—perhaps even more talented—than you. And they are probably more than a little peeved when a project goes to an outside source (i.e., you). Instead of competing with them, make them an advocate for your work and learn from their experience of the organization. Involve them in kick-off meetings, interview them to hear their opinions, run a co-creation workshop, and ensure that when the time comes to present the work to a client, they are already on your side.

BE TRANSPARENT, EVEN WHEN IT HURTS

On almost every project there will be a moment when there is bad news to tell the client. Perhaps you know that a printing cost is going to run over budget, or something is going to take longer than originally expected. Don't try and cover it up—proactively flag the problem and have a suggested solution on hand.

MAKE THEM LOOK GOOD

Help your client look good in front of their boss by factoring in time for things like the occasional stakeholder presentation. Proactively offering to put together a presentation of your work in a way that will appeal to their boss goes a long way in building a great client relationship. Remember, the creative industries are service industries, and it's amazing how far a little extra customer service will go.

HANDLING DIFFICULT CLIENTS

NON-DECIDER
The client who can't make any decisions

→ Provide clear recommendations and rationale every time you present work

KNOW-IT-ALL
They think they can do it all themselves

→ Take them aside and explain your process and the benefits of it

CHEAPSKATE
Won't pay for extra rounds of work

→ Enforce the contract details line-for-line. No favors for these types of clients

ASSHOLE
Rude or disrespectful to you or your team

→ Fired

SURVIVE YOUR FIRST BURNOUT

While a career in the creative industries might not seem as hazardous to one's health as some other occupations—say, for example, lion taming, snake milking, base jumping, or shark dentistry—it is not entirely without health risks. This is especially true when it comes to matters of the mind, specifically the infamous curse of the industry: creative burnout.

Now, I am not your doctor, your psychiatrist, or even your mother, so far be it from me to lecture you on matters of health. But even if you are a truly work-focussed sadist with a flagrant disregard for your personal wellbeing, let me tell you this: Aside from being bad for your health, creative burnout is also the enemy of great work.

BURNOUT IN THE CREATIVE INDUSTRIES

The creative industries have always had a pretty poor reputation when it comes to overwork and resulting burnout. Long hours driven by unrealistic deadlines and toxic culture, combined with the naturally insecure personalities of young creatives, have historically produced work environments that push people to their mental limits.

Take, for example, the sobering statistic that people in the creative industries are three times more likely than others to suffer from depression[7]. Or the tragic case of Matsuri Takahashi, the young advertising recruit who committed suicide after working more than 100 hours of overtime[8]. In short, burnout in the creative industries is a very real problem, and one that is often bizarrely celebrated as a badge of dedication to one's craft.

People in the creative industries are three times more likely than others to suffer from depression.

Let's be clear: Continually working long hours does not make you a better creative. It does not make you more dedicated. Above all else, it does not make you produce better work. That unsolved task that frustrates you until 3 a.m.? It will probably be done in a fraction of the time when you are fresh the next morning. Trust me.

ARE YOU HEADING FOR A CREATIVE BURNOUT?

I get it: You're just out of university and hungry for the hustle. You have boundless energy and give zero fucks about burnout—after all, you haven't even started yet. You survived university; how could you possibly be heading for a burnout? Keep this in mind: The creative industries have a habit of burning out people, even at the start of their career. If any of the items below sound familiar, chances are you're on track to a burnout.

---

[7] https://www.bbc.co.uk/news/uk-northern-ireland-foyle-west-43514255
[8] https://www.theguardian.com/world/2017/oct/05/japanese-woman-dies-overwork-159-hours-overtime

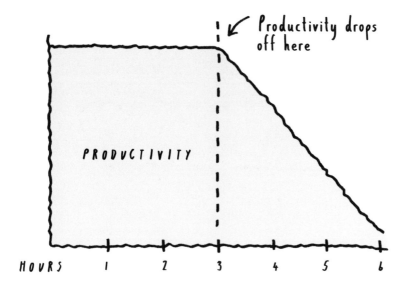

Productivity drops off here

PRODUCTIVITY

HOURS   1   2   3   4   5   6

YOU REGULARLY WORK MORE THAN 40 HOURS A WEEK

If you regularly work late nights every day of the week and expect to remain at peak productivity, you're kidding yourself. A Bureau of Labor study[9] shows that on average humans are productive for just under three hours per day. This is simple science, and everyone knows you don't mess with science.

YOU WORK MOST WEEKENDS

When it comes to your main job—regardless of whether you are freelance or full-time, one thing is clear: You should not be working weekends on your "day job." Of course, occasionally working a weekend for a deadline or a pitch is fine, but if it is happening more than once every couple of months, there is a problem.

Having mental space for creative play is essential to personal creative development.

YOU DON'T HAVE TIME OR ENERGY FOR A SIDE PROJECT (OR A LIFE)

Pay attention to this if you don't care about personal wellbeing but only about producing great work. In case you skipped 'Start a side hustle' (page 83), having mental space for creative play—also known as a side hustle—is essential to personal creative development. A sure sign of being overworked is coming home with zero energy or enthusiasm to even think about a side project. And if you're not pushing yourself to learn new skills on the side, your creative relevance will quickly fall behind.

[9] https://www.inc.com/melanie-curtin/in-an-8-hour-day-the-average-worker-is-productive-for-this-many-hours.html

THE BURNOUT CALCULATOR

In the past month, how many times did you:

Work more than 50 hours in a week?

Work over the weekend?

Have to cancel a social event for work?

Have to reply to work emails at midnight?

Feel overwhelmed and struggle to keep on top of your tasks?

RESULTS

0-1: Normal busy creative life

2-3: You need to get support

4+:   Fast track to burnout

AVOIDING AND MANAGING BURNOUT

It is this author's opinion that those managing creative teams are responsible for creating sustainable work environments, and that those who do not do so should be thrown to the lions, wolves, killer penguins, or something equally unpleasant.

However, the reality is that long hours are simply the status quo for many working in the creative industries, especially in sectors such as advertising, video-game design, and others. While there are positive signs of the creative industries shifting away from the unsustainable model, change happens slowly and the "churn and burn" model is still prevalent.

The good news is that, regardless of your level of seniority or the work environment you're in, there are some things that you can do to help avoid a burnout, even as a junior creative:

WORK SMARTER, NOT LONGER
There is no reason to be the last one out of the studio every night just to impress a creative director. Make a point of leaving at a reasonable time every day. Remember, you need to impress people with your work, not how many hours you're in the office.

Take a leaf out of the book of the Northern Europeans. Unlike the English-speaking Western nations such as the US and UK, in Northern Europe, long hours are strongly frowned upon: and those who frequently work them are seen as less competent for not getting their work done in the assigned time. For example, in the Berlin office of our agency, the doors are locked every day at 6.30 p.m. Unless you're in upper management with key privileges, you have to leave. Much like a bar after last orders, there is literally a person who walks around and sweeps everyone out.

DON'T BE AFRAID TO SAY NO
Unfortunately, all too often, young creatives have themselves to blame for their own burnouts. Creative directors will push and push in the name of great work, and young creatives simply are afraid to say no, or too caught up in the pursuit of "great work" to push back.

The reality is that most creative directors are not assholes, and probably don't realize the number of hours you're working to complete the tasks they've assigned you. For example, we recently had an extremely dedicated intern who was producing flawless work and never missed a deadline. What became apparent only after a routine check of her timesheets was that she had been working more than ten-hour days to get the work done but had not spoken up. We immediately shifted her workload to a normal level, and kept a close eye that she didn't burn herself out.

Here is a secret tip: Just say no. If you are working endless long hours, send the creative director a polite email explaining that while you are eager to produce great work, you are working 60 hours a week, and this is not sustainable on a personal or professional level. If you are working in an environment where there is a culture that discourages saying "no" to long hours, it is a clear sign to get the hell out of there.

DO NOT EAT LUNCH AT YOUR DESK

This seems like a no-brainer, yet it is something I see junior creatives doing day after day when they start a new job. Reality check: You need a break in the middle of the day, otherwise you will produce shit work. If you eat lunch at your desk in front of your computer, you are not resetting your brain. You will get stuck on the most simple task because your brain is tired. You will switch off at 3 p.m. and become about as useful as a turnip, or another equally non-creative root vegetable. Take an actual break.

REMEMBER, IT'S ONLY A JOB

There are no real emergencies. Put down your laptop. Go outside, get some fresh air, and speak to some other humans.

When it inevitably gets too much for you—and I promise you, every young creative will have burnout of some kind—remember this: It is just a job. A fun job, a rewarding job, yes, but still just a job. You are not a brain surgeon. You are not a firefighter. You are not saving the world. Whether you are making ads for fizzy water, designing logos for cans of fruit, making clothes for the wealthy, or filming the most hilarious cat video the world has ever seen, you are still working in the creative industries. There are no real emergencies. Put down your laptop. Go outside, get some fresh air, and speak to some other humans.

THE WELLBEING CHECKLIST*

☐ I will not eat lunch at my desk

☐ I will not work more than 40 hours a week

☐ I will not sit in front of my computer like a cave troll for 16 hours per day

☐ I will not reply to emails at midnight

☐ I will learn to switch off

☐ I will learn to say "no"

☐ I will actually say "no"

☐ I will tell people to piss off if they ignore me when I say "no"

☐ I will clear enough time in my week to have a side project (or personal life)

☐ I will remember that I am not a surgeon and there are no real "creative emergencies"

*Be prepared to ignore these rules from time to time

MAKE A BIG CHANGE

There comes a time in every creative career when you will need to abandon the comfort and safety of your current situation and make a big change. Relinquish the signature style that you have used forever. Quit the prestigious agency job you've held for five years. Pack your entire life into a suitcase and move to a new country. Change is the secret to professional growth in the creative industries— where producing fresh and innovative output is paramount to continuing to get work in the door. So, how do you know when it's time to reset, reinvent, or restart? Read on.

WHY CHANGE IS IMPORTANT

A few years ago, I worked alongside a tremendously talented art director—let us call him Cedric Crofflemeister—who had been at the agency for about five years. He was one of those gems who everyone wanted to work with. His concepts were brilliantly original, his execution was flawless, and above all, he was a pleasure to work with. Just about every award-winning project that came out of the agency had his fingerprints on it. He was adored by the designers who worked with him, he commanded respect and influence among senior management, and, unsurprisingly, he was extremely well paid.

One Monday morning, the team came into the studio and noticed that Cedric's desk was empty. He could not be found in the photography studio or the kitchen, or even lurking around the beer storage closet. That afternoon, a note was sent around from the group creative director informing everyone that Cedric had abruptly decided to leave the agency world behind. Not only had he handed in his notice, he had sold his car, and moved out of his apartment, and was now renting a live-in studio space with the single-minded vision of becoming an artist. Needless to say, everyone in the agency thought Cedric had lost his mind.

Within two years of quitting his agency job, Cedric's drawings started appearing in the columns of *The New Yorker*. His paintings were popping up in galleries all over the city, and he was being interviewed by just about every creative publication out there. In short, he made a ballsy move—exiting an extremely cushy position in a well-respected agency—but it paid off. Big time.

Change forces us out of our comfort zone. It makes us uncomfortable. But here's the thing: Change also pushes us to do things that surprise us. It makes us capable of doing things that we didn't think we were capable of. And once it starts, this new-found confidence has a snowball effect. We start to get bolder, taking more risks and, from a creative perspective, producing more exciting work.

IS IT TIME FOR A CHANGE?

HOW DO YOU FEEL ABOUT YOUR CURRENT ROLE?

| IT'S NO LONGER FUN AND I FEEL CREATIVELY STUCK | I LOVE THE ROLE, BUT MY WORK IS REPEATING ITSELF | COOL WORK, FUN PLACE, BUT I'M STILL SCARED SHITLESS |

IS THERE A STRONG PERSONAL OR FINANCIAL REASON TO STAY PUT?

WILL THIS ROLE ADD FRESH WORK TO YOUR PORTFOLIO IN THE NEXT YEAR?

ARE YOU SUPPORTED WITH MENTORSHIP OF SOME KIND TO HELP YOU GROW?

NO   YES   NO   YES   NO   YES

CHANGE WHERE YOU WORK

If you are stuck in a creative rut or not getting the support you need for growth, it might be the time to change roles.

CHANGE HOW YOU WORK

Mixing things up is the key to fresh work. Change your desk, work in a brand-new style, or try a completely new process.

STAY PUT FOR NOW

It sounds like you're in a good role doing interesting work. Keep the personal growth with constant learning.

RECOGNIZING THAT YOU NEED A CHANGE

Knowing when the time is right to make a big change is tricky. On the one hand, you don't want to become stuck in a dead-end role, but on the other, you don't want to proverbially "throw the baby out with the bathwater" either. For example, don't quit a perfectly good job just because you had a bad month with a difficult creative director.

While there is no one-size-fits-all rule when it comes to making a change, there are a few tell-tale signs that indicate when it may be time to shake things up:

YOU FEEL OVERLY COMFORTABLE IN WHAT YOU'RE DOING
You've been working in a job for a few years with a good salary, nice colleagues, and easy clients. Feeling well and truly settled in, you are comfortable that you've seen it all and can handle everything this job can throw at you. Above all, you no longer feel uncomfortable or scared. Sound familiar? It's probably a sign that you're too comfortable in your position, and it's time to make a change.

> The most visible sign that you need to change something in your projects, your process, or your life is when repetition starts to appear in your work.

I had this realization after about four years of living and working in Berlin. At the time, I loved everything about the city, from the winding cobbled streets with the Sunday farmers' markets, to the parties that would run all the way through the weekends—it was a great place to call home. Not only that, but I had a great job at a well-known design agency with fantastic projects, clients, and teams.

Around early 2014, I realized that I was stuck. I had become too comfortable in my role—I was in my late twenties and almost five of those years had been at the same agency. I knew that in order to push my career and work forward, I needed a new experience and place. And so, I packed my bags and moved to New York.

YOU'RE STARTING TO REPEAT STYLES AND IDEAS FROM OLD WORK
For creatives, the most visible sign that you need to change something in your projects, your process, or your life is when repetition starts to appear

in your work. At some stage or another, this happens to every creative, regardless of level of experience, age, or how successful you are. Sure, it's OK to have a signature style, but even those with the most recognizable styles need to evolve over time.

Arrange a retrospective of your projects every six months and analyze the work. Using the approach of the American designer Tibor Kalman, ask yourself: Have I already used the same type of approach more than three times? If the answer is yes, it's time to try something completely different.

YOU FALL BACK INTO THE SAME PROCESS FOR EVERY PROJECT

In the creative industries, having a "set" process can be a great thing. It means that you can get a project up and running quickly and efficiently, and the right process ensures a reliable result every time. But for all the same reasons, there comes a time when the same process can also be a noose that makes everything look the same. If you're falling into the same five steps for project after project, it is probably time to shake things up before your work starts to look tired.

Do something that makes you uncomfortable every day.

HOW TO MAKE A CHANGE

Before you quit your job and abandon your family to be a llama trainer in Peru, it's probably an idea to try a smaller change in your day-to-day work. Here are some ideas to shake things up, from small to large:

DO SOMETHING THAT MAKES YOU UNCOMFORTABLE EVERY DAY

In the words of the nineteenth-century lecturer, philosopher, and purveyor of fantastic sideburns Ralph Waldo Emerson, "always do what you are afraid to do." And in the words of just about every self-help book under the sun, do something that makes you uncomfortable every day. Referring to the notion of "creative play" from the "Start a side hustle" chapter, the creative mind expands only when you do something new.

For example:
-Shit at drawing? Get a sketchbook and draw something.
-Use a new design tool instead of the one you've used for the past ten years.
-Afraid of public speaking? Force yourself to do regular presentations.

The list is endless. Pick something that makes you uncomfortable and do it every day.

DROP YOUR SIGNATURE STYLE

Once you land on a signature style and start to gain traction with it—whether as a designer, illustrator, photographer, or filmmaker—it becomes exceedingly difficult to change it. You've had a taste of success with a certain way of doing things, so why change now? The truth is that no style or approach—no matter how good—is impervious to time. Staying relevant as a creative means reinventing yourself again and again.

Take a look at the most successful musicians of the past 100 years—the Beatles, David Bowie, Madonna—the list goes on. What sets them apart in terms of longevity? The constant pursuit of reinvention. As hard as it might be, do your future self a favor and be ready to reinvent yourself every couple of years. Explore a new medium. Deconstruct your process and do everything in reverse order. Use your hands, or, if you already do, stop using them and use a computer. Take a walk. Change all the furniture in your office space. Visit an art gallery. Meditate. It doesn't matter what you do—just do something different.

> Do not spend more than two to three years in any one company during the first ten years of your career.

CHANGE JOB EVERY THREE YEARS (AT LEAST AT THE BEGINNING)

Assuming smaller changes haven't worked, it's time to consider something more dramatic. Changing your job may be something to consider.

On the subject of changing jobs, let me tell you something a recruiter or career counselor never will: Do not spend more than two to three years in any one company during the first ten years of your career. There is only so much you can learn at one company. This is particularly true in the early years of your career, when you need to act like a human sponge, soaking up as many diverse and different perspectives and influences as possible.

MOVE TO A NEW CITY OR COUNTRY

Perhaps the most radical way to make a change is to move to a new city—or, better still, a whole new country. Nothing presses the reset button in your mindset, your work, and your life more than travel. The more radical the cultural difference, the better. Travel opens up the creative mind like nothing else. You should move country at least once (but preferably at least three times) in your career. You can read more about travel in the creative industries on page 94.

MOVING ON

No matter how hard it might seem, no matter how many people say you're crazy to leave, or what your mom says, never be afraid to make a big change. Or, to put it more accurately: You should be scared shitless of making a change, but do it anyway. Change is the catalyst for learning, that secret sauce that keeps our minds sharp and our creative output fresh, unexpected, and occasionally brilliant. It is that fear, that uncertainty about the unknown, that is a required element of producing brilliant creative work, and that keeps us on our proverbial toes.

As you take the plunge into the start of your career, it may seem that you have a mountain to climb and an ocean of things to learn. In truth, the path to mastering your craft never ends. You see, at the very top of the Shit They Didn't Tell You list is that you will never—no matter how hard you try—really figure it all out.

> Change is the catalyst for learning, that secret sauce that keeps our minds sharp and our creative output fresh, unexpected, and occasionally brilliant.

The creative industries are a limitless plane of unknowns, of unseen challenges, hidden opportunities, shortcuts, long cuts, and side paths that terrify and delight at the same time. There is no straight path. There is no map. We're all beginners. We all know jack shit. The very best creatives are those who never stop wanting to get lost along the way, take a detour, and strive to find that next big thing that no one ever dreamed was possible.

And that's what makes the whole thing so damn fun in the first place.

THE GRADUATE MANIFESTO

1. I will make a plan
2. I will be ready to ignore that plan when a great opportunity appears
3. I will invest the time to find my own creative voice
4. I will present my work in a focussed way
5. I will find a mentor
6. I will not miss deadlines
7. I will start a side hustle
8. I will work abroad at least once
9. I will at least try to understand the business side of the creative industries
10. I will try to work normal hours
11. I will actively look for ways to make my workplace more diverse and inclusive
12. I will not be afraid to make a big change
13. I will never stop being curious
14. I will ignore the rules (including this rule)

CUT OUT AND HANG IN YOUR SPACE

ACKNOWLEDGMENTS

While it may seem that the very notion of this book is taking aim *against* creative education, that really couldn't be farther from the truth. In our age, when knowledge is more democratized than ever, creative education is better, and more accessible, than ever. It seems that the gap between education and practice is closing, albeit slowly.

I've been very lucky with my own creative education. I want to make a special mention of the incredible staff at Technological University Dublin, who provided me with a creatively rich and varied—while still practical—education. To John Short, Tom Kelly, Brenda Dermody, Anita Heavey, Brenda Duggan, Clare Bell, Mary Ann Bolger, Ann Creavin, Barry Sheehan, Kieran Corcoran, Louise Reddy, Peter Dee, Tom Grace, Peter Jones, and all the other great lecturers at the university, thank you. Your guidance and support made me the designer I am today. From my Master's degree, I would like to mention Peter Smith for all his patience in putting up with what was an extremely unfocussed and difficult student.

On the topic of education, this section would not be complete without a mention of Professor Sam Anvari from California State University, Long Beach, who continually goes above and beyond to bring the "real industry" into the classroom. Sam and I have collaborated on the school's UI/UX program, focussing on giving students a sense of the real world through continuous industry collaboration and real-life briefs.

Outside of traditional education, I want to say a big thank you to the mentors and friends I've been lucky enough to have throughout my career: Professional provocateur Erik Spiekermann, who has been a friend and guide for many years; Ray Doyle from Brand Social and Steven Cook at Edenspiekermann Berlin, my mentors in the early days during my respective internships. And a special thanks to Chris Do for helping with the foreword for this book.

In the creative industries, learning never stops. I want to take a moment and thank our incredible team at Edenspiekermann, whose endless enthusiasm and drive to create great work is a testament to the importance of constantly pushing oneself into new and unfamiliar territory to stay creatively fresh.

This section would not be complete without mentioning the amazing group of people at Laurence King who have believed enough in this little series of vulgar books to publish a second title, which you now hold in your hands. A million thanks to Laurence, Gaynor, Liz, Kara, Anastasia, Max, Sabine, Alison, Barney, Angela and Chris at TurnbullGrey, and all the co-edition publishers around the world.

Last, but certainly not least, I want to thank the people who enabled me to do this whole thing in the first place—my family. Thanks to all of you, especially my gran, Mick, mom, and my wife, Nora, for putting up with me this whole time. You rock.

A closing note to the design leaders, agencies, and creative directors reading these words: After you close this little guide, reach out to your local university. Better still, reach out to one that is underfunded, works with underrepresented groups, or needs support. Offer to run a course there. Give them a real brief. Go in and do a lecture. Set up an internship program. Creative courses at universities live or die by providing an education that is industry-relevant—and that can only come from collaboration with active participation from practitioners. Together, the future of creative education, and the responsibility to create a more diverse, equal, and inclusive industry, is in our hands. Make your influence count.

About the Author

Paul Woods is a Los Angeles-based designer and writer. He leads Edenspiekermann's creative and technology teams as CEO, building products, brands, and service-design work for clients in industries such as editorial, sustainability, and transportation.

Over the course of his career, Paul has been at the helm of projects for Red Bull, Google, Faraday Future, The City of Santa Monica, and Morgan Stanley, among many others. An advocate for the importance of user-centric design, Paul places a hyper-focus on the user in his work. A thought leader in the design and technology spaces, his bylines regularly appear in publications such as *Fast Company*, *AdWeek*, and *The Drum*.

In his spare time, Paul is a writer, illustrator, and co-founder of the satirical industry website *Adloids*. His first book, *How to Do Great Work Without Being an Asshole*, was released worldwide in 2019 by Laurence King and is available in more than eight languages.

Paul lives in Pasadena with his wife, Nora, and a very stubborn basset hound. www.paulthedesigner.us